C2 869293 00 25

D1346288

WITHDRAWN FROM
NEWCASTLE UPON TYNE
CITY LIBRARIES

# Newcastle
City Council

## Newcastle Libraries and Information Service
### Fines may be charged for late returns
Please return or renew this item by the last date shown. Books can be
renewed at the library, by post or by telephone if not reserved by another reader.

| Due for return | Due for return | Due for return |
| --- | --- | --- |
| - 9 JAN 2006 | | |
| - 2 FEB 2006 | | |
| 2 3 MAY 2006 | | |
| 19 June 6. | | |
| 2 1 SEP 2006 | | |
| 2 5 FEB 2008 | | |
| - 2 APR 2008 | | |
| - 3 JUN 2008 | | |
| - 1 JUL 2008 | | |
| 1 7 JUL 2009 | | |
| 0 4 DEC 2010 | | |

# MARY GILLIATT'S
# Home Comforts with Style

# MARY GILLIATT'S
# Home Comforts with Style

## A DECORATING GUIDE FOR TODAY'S LIVING

### Photographs by Andreas von Einsiedel

CONRAN
OCTOPUS

First published in 2004 by Watson-Guptill Publications
a division of VNU Business Media, Inc.,
770 Broadway, New York, N.Y. 10003
www.watsonguptill.com

This edition published in 2005 by Conran Octopus Ltd
a part of Octopus Publishing Group
2–4 Heron Quays, London E14 4JP
www.conran-octopus.co.uk

Text copyright © 2004 Mary Gilliatt
Photographs copyright © 2004 Andreas von Einsiedel

Senior Acquisitions Editor: Victoria Craven
Project Editor: Andrea Curley
Designer: Areta Buk/Thumb Print
Production Manager: Hector Campbell

All rights reserved. No part of this publication may be reproduced, stored in a retrieval system or transmitted in any form or by any means, electronic, electrostatic magnetic tape, mechanical, photocopying, recording, or otherwise, without the prior permission of the Publisher.

ISBN 1 84091 433 5

British Library Cataloguing-in-Publication Data. A catalogue record for this book is available from the British Library.

Printed in Singapore

| NEWCASTLE UPON TYNE CITY LIBRARIES | |
| --- | --- |
| C2 869293 OO 25 | |
| Askews | Jun-2005 |
| 747 | £20.00 |
| | |

*For my three children:*
*Sophia Gilliatt, Tom Gilliatt, and Annie Constantine,*
*who are all very good at producing comfortable and interesting homes.*

## ACKNOWLEDGMENTS

Once again it has been a pleasure to work with the particularly nice team at Watson-Guptill, and I wish to record my special thanks to Victoria Craven, who commissioned this book on comfort and who goes out of her way to be as helpful as she can; to Andrea Curley for editing it so patiently and tactfully; to Areta Buk for designing it; to Hector Campbell for producing it; to Lee Wiggins for publicizing it; and to Bob Ferro for overseeing the lot.

On the home front, I am grateful to Mike Adams for being so understanding and coming to my aid when required; to Jane Turner for always so comfortingly "being there" at difficult times and difficult hours; and to my older granddaughters, Olivia and Georgia Constantine, for being gratifyingly enthusiastic about their grandmother's books.

# Contents

# INTRODUCTION Comfort in Today's World

BELOW: *Comfort is subjective, and how one makes their home "comfortable" is a matter of personal taste. Some find comfort in simple, serene settings, like the one pictured here, bathed in sunlight with a generous display of fresh flowers.*

OPPOSITE: *No matter how downy soft the comforter or pillow may be, a bedroom will not feel completely comfortable if the overall atmosphere of the room—the furniture arrangement, the color scheme—is not pleasurable. This all-white setting is visually soothing and invites repose.*

MOST OF US HAVE ALWAYS WANTED and needed shelter and as we prospered, have felt the need to embellish and decorate that shelter; but actual home and creature comforts have rarely assumed the priority that they do now. As the outside world gets more precarious and unpredictable, as former certainties seem far less certain, we seem to need our homes to be comfortable and comforting as never before. If living well is the best revenge, as was said in the 1920s after the ravages of World War I, most of us now seem to accept that living comfortably adds a soothing solidity, a sense of continuity, a solace and feeling of well-being to our lives that appears to be increasingly essential.

But comfort is not a concise word—it has no one precise meaning. And it is as much emotional as physical, as subconscious as it is conscious. Hear the word and it can conjure up a warm, cozy vision, or a cool, fresh vision, depending upon where you are and in what season. But what is comfortable and what is comforting are highly subjective. One person's comfort is another's discomfort, for comfort by no means depends upon luxury or sumptuousness, although it is often equated with the two. Many people find comfort in total simplicity, things that are spare and natural and serve their purpose well. Others find comfort in anything that is casual and informal and relaxed. Some people find comfort in a home that is as "perfect" as it is possible to be. Others find an obvious striving for perfection in a room something

akin to a straightjacket. Still others find a comfort in the familiar, the settled, the nostalgic, the predictability of ritual. They only accept the new and different with reluctance until, with use, these too become familiar and comfortable.

Clearly then comfort is a compendium in general: a portmanteau word covering many different emotions, feelings, and takes on the subject. For example, however *physically* comfortable a bed, a sofa, or a chair, it will feel that much more easeful and gratifying if it is agreeable to look at, if the mind is at rest and not jangled, and if there is nothing in the atmosphere of the room, even the level of light or the temperature, to jar the general pleasure. So in many ways, real *all-around* comfort is a balancing act between things working well, feeling comfortable and looking good, and the state of mind of the user.

That, I think, is what most people nowadays would like to create in a home, what most people, indeed, would always want no matter what new discoveries, aids, and additions to comfort there may be. They want to create a truly all-around comfortable *shelter* from the outside world. That, together with a degree of personal stylishness or idiosyncrasy. Comfort of all sorts with style. Style with comfort. Style that is comforting.

And this book sets out to show the various ways to make real comfort in the home achievable in conjunction with the subliminal comforts that have always been desired. And when I say various ways, I mean it. Wherever appropriate I have explained how to bring lighting to its most comfortable level for every situation; how to choose the most comforting and comfortable colors for room schemes; how to organize the sort of storage that makes for maximum convenience and neatness; how to decide on the right flooring and window treatments; and how to arrange furniture and accessories for maximum ease and enjoyment. In short, I have tried to show that rather than a didactic right way and a wrong way to decorate and furnish, there are *comfortable* ways and less comfortable ways depending on where and how you live.

## Comfort Zoning
### FIRST ATTEND TO THE BASICS

Before launching into any specifics on the art, or arts, of comfort, it is important to emphasize that the first task in any home, in any room, if you want real background comfort with the minimum of hardware, so to speak, is to get the temperature, insulation, wiring, and lighting as right as possible. If any of these basics need to be updated, altered, or indeed, added (and can be afforded, which is an important point to consider) they should be planned for and installed before any other work is undertaken. Clearly in cool climates you should be concerned with getting the warmth right. In warm climates you should focus on keeping the place as cool as you can. Both tasks are made immeasurably easier by modern insulation to reduce energy consumption and unnecessary damage to the environment. The ideal is to have heat or cooling sources that are as invisible as possible, which means either having in-ceiling or under-floor heating, or a central ducted warm (or cool) air system with small, neat grilles for outlets. Furniture layouts should be worked out so that sofas and large pieces of furniture are not placed in front of such grilles, or registers, or the heat (or cool air) will be wasted.

And if you use a designer, take your time to choose one. Make sure that you are quite comfortable with his or her manner, taste, and range of knowledge. Empathy is all-important.

# Extending a Warm Welcome

*The need for a welcoming hall has become a decorational cliché, but like all clichés it contains a much-repeated truth. Opening the door from the outside world into a hall should be a psychological comfort and as interesting a foretaste of what is to come as it is beguiling.*

If you think of what a home is for, it should be an axiom that the more emphasis there is on making family and friends feel relaxed and at ease, and quite literally at home immediately, the more comforting and therefore the more memorable it will be. And this feeling should be set as soon as a guest steps through the doorway of your home.

An entrance hall should be as easy as possible on the eye. It should be a space that smells at least fresh if not delicious, or even, if the ambiance is right, exotically delicious. And it should be a space that puts the emphasis on comfort and harmony rather than on impressiveness.

If the hall is already naturally impressive architecturally, then that impressiveness should be tempered with as much sense of domestic ease as is possible. And grandeur *can* be softened—by lighting, colors, rugs, accessories, and comfortable-*looking*, as well as comfortable-*feeling*, seating.

The preponderance of halls and hallways, however, are small and dark rather than grand, and sometimes they are so small that there is no way that any furniture can be fitted in. In any case, a really comfortable-looking space, or at least a space, however small, that looks as if it is going to lead one on to charming and interesting rooms, is generally impressive in its own right. In these halls, the onus of comfort is carried by lighting, colors, floor covering, and accessories.

ABOVE: *A comfortable hall, however small, should hint of the charm to be found throughout all the rooms of the home. An attractive arrangement of prints or photographs and potted flowering plants lend character and interest.*

LEFT: *When considering hallways, it is important that the lighting, colors, flooring, and accessories harmonize as one's eye is led from room to room. Smooth visual transitions serve to make a home feel in accord.*

OPPOSITE: *Even if the hall is architecturally impressive, the grandeur can be softened with whimsical touches. Here, a classical bust loses its severity dressed up in a wide-rimmed hat and scarf.*

# Creating a Memorable Hallway

## LIGHTING

Not many halls have windows, especially in apartment buildings. Therefore, left to themselves with only the modicum of lighting, they can look gloomy. Moreover, since some people, and most younger family members, tend to leave things around in a hall, regardless of house rules or aesthetics, the lighting should be good enough to prevent the unwary from accidentally tripping over unexpected objects. Although it is hard to follow councils of perfection when there are small children and teenagers around, at least you can establish a comfortable, cheerful framework that will look good and work well once offending objects have been removed.

Staircases and landings too need to be well-lit at all times with light directed on to the floor to show any changes in levels (you might be familiar with the odd step down to another room but your visitors won't be), and light directed to the walls to show switches and door handles. So, for the various areas to be comfortable enough to move around in without any fear of accidents, the lighting has to be well-thought-out. Stairs, for example, are safest when lit at the top and bottom of the flight (see "Light for Night," page 15). Hall closets should have an internal light that will go on automatically when the door is opened, or else an angled light on the ceiling outside to avoid a constant irritating grope in the dark for coats. And in the case of a dark hall and staircase, the ideal is to have different light sources for the day and for the night. The reason is that it is much more cheerful not to see an obvious light fixture on during the daylight hours.

## Comfort Zoning

### LIGHTING BASICS

All changes or installation of new wiring should be done *before* decoration and not as an afterthought. This stricture, of course, applies as well to any other sort of wiring for security systems, cable TV, telephone lines, computers, and so on. It sounds so elemental, but it is extraordinary how often this is forgotten.

*The lighting in a hall should be good enough that any odd objects lying about are clearly visible. Stairs and landings should also be well-lit, with the light directed onto the floor to prevent any missteps.*

# Concealing Artificial Light During the Day

The sight of lightbulbs switched on during what should be daylight hours often makes you feel more daylight-deprived rather than less. It makes it so much more cheerful if you can conceal light sources wherever possible.

- Conceal strings of small lightbulbs or the kind of fluorescent tubes that are the nearest to daylight behind soffits or cornices between wall and ceiling, placed slightly raised in order to allow room for the fixtures.
- If there is a window, have a light source behind a pelmet above the window, or light sources behind shutters that are half closed so that at least it *looks* as if it is an agreeable day outside.
- Up-lights concealed in corners and behind plants or pieces of furniture are a sensible and more inexpensive way of providing less obvious artificial light.
- Halogen bulbs in tall sculptural-looking lamps give a big punch of light with no sight of a bulb as there would be in a conventional lamp or a light with a shade. Placed on either side of a window in a dark space, if there is room, they will increase the illusion of light coming in naturally.
- A suspended luminous ceiling (with concealed light above) will give a much sunnier feeling in a dark hall, as long as it is supplemented at night by some other light source. Otherwise it will be too bland.
- Run strips of tiny bulbs above baseboards in halls, and on staircases and landings. Or recess small square or round light fixtures low along the bottoms of walls or to the sides of stair treads.

*Up-lights concealed in corners or behind plants create an agreeable, soft atmosphere in both daytime and evening. Large, sculptural-looking lamps can also bathe a room in light without the unpleasant distraction of a conspicuous bulb.*

**LIGHT FOR NIGHT**

Night is the time, of course, when you *can* show off the lights. And they should be controlled by separate switches and never used in conjunction with any fluorescent tubes that you might have used to supplement daylight. This is because, in my opinion, the general softness of tungsten light does not mix well with the brighter light of fluorescence however much more sophisticated and user-friendly it has become.

Other than that you could just supplement any other daylight aids with a table lamp or two if the space is big enough to have any surfaces on which to stand them, because such lamps always look friendly and, by definition, comforting as you come in. In any event, if you have a telephone in the hall, there should be light beside it. Try always to use three-way bulbs so light intensity can be varied if the lamps do not have a separate circuit to allow them to be controlled from a dimmer switch by the door.

If you have a central ceiling outlet or outlets, this is the place to make use of them. By all means find good-looking hall lanterns or chandeliers, whether

## Comfort Zoning

### HALLWAY SAFETY BASICS

Halls, stairs, corridors, and landings can be especially dangerous
if there are very young, very old,
or very nearsighted members of
a household. If you are not sure
what, if any, area is underlit, walk
around at dusk (taking due care
yourself, of course) with the house
or apartment unlit. And even if
your own eyes are perfectly sound
and sharp, remember that eyes
deteriorate with age, so that the
average sixty-year-old needs twice
as much light as the average thirty-
year-old, and what seems tolerably
safe to a healthy adult might not
be so for the elderly—or for small
children, who might also be afraid
of the dark.

*If there are windows, supple-
ment the light that comes in
naturally with table lamps and
other light sources, so that even
if the day is dreary it at least
appears to be agreeable outside.*

antique, retro, or modern, but attach them to dimmer switches so that you can
alter the level of lighting as and when you please. These too look good dimmed
to a comfortable level and used with concealed up-lights, also dimmed, to light
up corners and to throw light onto the ceiling.

If you have art or objects to show off, the ideal lighting is recessed low-voltage
angled spots, wall washers, or down-lights, again on dimmer switches. However,
place them judiciously, rather than riddle the ceiling with them, about 2 to 3 feet
(.6 to 1 m) out from the walls, to get a good wash or a more precise angle,
depending upon whether you are using wall washers or spots and are lighting a
whole arrangement of prints or paintings or just one or two.

Comfortable lighting for stairs should obviously emphasize safety, so try to
keep all treads and risers lit. (If you have installed recessed squares or circular
minilights to the sides of the stairs, so much the better.) Otherwise, it is good to
install a recessed down-light or some sort of light at the head of the stairs so that
the risers are in a fair amount of shadow but the treads and their projecting edges,
or nosiness, are accentuated. To avoid having *too* much shadow on the risers, and
to show distinctly where the last tread ends, there should also be another light at
the bottom of a flight. If recessed ceiling or pendant lights don't work with the
lay of the ceiling, you could install wall lights instead. If you have small children
or elderly guests around, it is a good idea to have all such lights on a dimmer
switch so that the lights can be dimmed during sleeping hours, so as not to disturb sleep or waste too much electricity, yet remain adequate for good vision.

## WINDOWS

If you have a window or windows in a hall, corridor, or landing, or on the stairs, look at them carefully to decide whether you should curtain them, shade them, shutter them, or put glass shelves over them to display, say, a collection of colored glass, especially if this will conceal the really depressing view that you sometimes get in town houses.

In general, unless you have very long and gracious windows, I would avoid curtains, which simply get in the way in these areas. Smaller windows look neater and let in more light if they are covered with shades or shutters or even some sort of grille. Very small windows are usually much better just left as is, with a plant, vase of flowers, or some sort of decorative object to cheer up the sill. French doors in a hallway are also usually best left to show off a yard or terrace, which can be lit at night (see pages 164–167). Use shutters and grilles placed at the sides for security—a cause for comfort in itself.

*If the windows in a hall, corridor, or landing, are graceful and generous, a curtain treatment like this one will work beautifully. But if the windows are on the small side, it is best to cover them with shutters or shades.*

## COLORS

Given that halls and staircases are often inclined to be on the dark side, it is a good idea to paint or otherwise decorate them in strong, rich colors, especially in cooler climates. Painting a dark or gloomy space in light colors in an effort to reverse the murkiness will only guarantee that you end up with a sort of dim grayish space—and not that tranquil, calm gray either, which, when spiced with pure white, looks marvelous in hot climates (see "Whites and Neutrals," page 110).

Strong, rich colors, on the other hand, provide an inviting shadowy warmth, however scarce the light. And even if you are nervous of using strong color, you must remember that this is a space that, on the whole, you are always passing *through*. You are not expected to hang around in it, unless, of course, the square footage is generous enough to allow for a dining or library hall. But there again, unless you live in the tropics, semitropics, or other generally sun-filled climates (where greens, blues, whites, and neutrals are more sensible), richer colors, especially in the reds and yellows range, are preferable.

## FLOORING

Comfort underfoot in hallways and on stairs is not just a literal comfort for the foot in a specific climate or location. To ensure a *general* sense of comfort, any floor covering in these areas also needs to be easy to clean, hard-wearing, long-lasting, appropriate to the area, and, because any floor covering that fills these various requirements is bound to be expensive, in a color that is neutral enough to withstand any radical changes in decorative schemes. Moreover, if a staircase or corridor leads out of the hall, it should be floored or carpeted in the same or at the very least coordinating colors.

Good quality carpeting—and it really must be good quality to endure the mostly heavy traffic in these areas—is obviously comfortable, and, depending on the price, sometimes downright luxurious; but it is definitely more suitable for townhouses and particularly for apartments in temperate climates than for country, suburban, and vacation homes. Where apartments are concerned, much of the outside dirt is walked off in the main entrance, the public areas, and the elevator, if there is one. Town houses can just get away with carpet if they have a large area of coconut matting placed in a shallow well just before the front door, with another generous mat outside, because mud and real dirt are less likely to be trailed indoors from town and city streets than from country and suburban roads and yards.

If a hall and staircase are not going to get an excessive amount of daily use or brought-in dirt, rush matting, sea grass, coir, and sisal look earthy and natural in both town and country houses. But avoid too slippery a variety of the last three on staircases (avoid rush matting altogether, as it would not be appropriate or practical). Any of the wool sisal varieties would avoid the slip problem and look good texturally. Do, however, combine wool sisal with serviceable front door coconut matting, as well as with natural coirs or sea grass rugs for both greater longevity and cleaning purposes.

Comfort Zoning
### WALL SURFACE BASICS

Whatever color you decide to use in your hall and staircase, if there is one (and this advice applies whether you use paint, fabric, or wallpaper), the walls must be hard-wearing. That is to say, the surfaces must be retouchable or patchable, since all the through-traffic, as well as the (occasional) moving in and out of furniture, packages, bicycles, strollers, and other accessories of family life, take their inevitable toll on walls.

ABOVE: *Hardwood floors are ideal for high traffic areas like hallways and stairs, as they are hard-wearing and easy to clean. If the flooring extends into rooms beyond the hallway, it should either match or coordinate in color and treatment.*

OPPOSITE: *Walls in halls should be painted in strong, rich colors, like this deep red, to provide warmth to an otherwise dark and dim space. Floor colors should be neutral to accommodate changes in color schemes.*

## Comfort Zoning
### FLOOR COVERING BASICS

When choosing a floor covering for the hall and staircase, remember to take into consideration transitions into other rooms opening off it. In smaller homes it is wise to consider one type of floor covering throughout to help enlarge the feeling of space. If you do have different floor coverings, make sure that colors don't jar. To keep the joins neat, install brass, nickel, or wood saddles across doorways.

Wood floors are a good choice in any sort of hall—perhaps combined with a good quality stair carpet—because they are hard-wearing, comparatively easy to clean, and neutral-colored, and they can be spiced up with rugs or a decorative runner, provided the latter is made slip-proof with the slightly sticky underlay, cut to fit, that is available from good carpet and rug stores. Lesser known woods such as hickory and pecan are just as durable but less expensive than red and white oaks, cherry, chestnut, and walnut. Australian Ironwood is as tough as, well, iron.

Nonslip ceramic, quarry, terra-cotta, marble, limestone, flagstone, slate, or granite tiles and bricks, especially old bricks, are cool in hot climates and can work in less amiable temperatures, especially in country houses, in conjunction with various rugs and kilims. And they are better still for real comfort, with under-floor heating. All of these heavier materials, however, will need solid or reinforced sub floors. Well-polished and sealed concrete can look handsome in modern buildings, especially when warmed with rugs in cool climates, and do not forget that concrete can also be painted in any design as long as it is properly prepared with a sealer and undercoat then given final coats of sealant or polyurethane. (For more on hard floors, see page 95.)

Although they are less expensive than any of the above materials, vinyl and linoleum (used in conjunction with stair carpeting in a house or duplex) can be inlaid and juxtaposed and bordered in all kinds of interesting designs.

Stone stairs, if you have them, are made more comfortable in cooler climates, though not necessarily more handsome or more easy to clean, by the addition of a carpet or runner. If you use carpeting on wood stairs, it is generally more satisfactory and certainly easier to clean if you run the carpet right across the treads.

## FURNITURE AND ACCESSORIES

However large or small a hall, its welcoming character will depend as much on the furniture, such as it is, and particularly on the accessories, as on the lighting, wall decoration, and floor covering. If space permits try to install at least one interesting chair and a big enough table to hold flowers or a plant, mail, possibly a telephone and telephone directories, and a space for keys and the other small paraphernalia that collect in this part of the home. And there should be a mirror

ABOVE: *Wood floors can be spiced up with runners, but the rugs will need to be made slip-proof with a sticky underlay. If space permits, a table or shelf with room enough to hold a plant, mail, keys, or telephone will make the hall as functional as it is welcoming.*

OPPOSITE: *Mirrors add wonderful sparkle to a landing, in addition to visually expanding the space. Paintings and prints add personality and cheer, as do small sculptures and collections of memorabilia.*

TOP: *When choosing furniture for an older home, it is best to keep within the spirit of the building. Ornate candelabra like those pictured above look quite stylish in this hallway.*

ABOVE: *A pedestal, urn, or piece of sculpture can look good in a corner or narrow hall. Decorative pieces can provide interest as well as color.*

for checking appearance both when coming in and going out (as well as for visually enlarging the space and for adding sparkle), an umbrella stand, and a generous closet for coats. If there is no space for a closet, there should at least be a coat rack or a row of pegs that is not too much in the mainstream of traffic (a row of disheveled outdoor wear is not the best-looking sight). If the space is too narrow for a table and chair, try putting in a bench or at the very least, a shelf. Of course if there is a window, the windowsill itself can often provide a necessary surface that will leave room, perhaps on the floor, for some decorative object such as an urn or a plant in a basket or planter.

If there is space for more, what sort of furniture you choose—and to my mind halls look better under- rather than over-furnished—depends naturally on the general style of your home, your tastes, and your pocket. If you have an old house, it is usually good to keep within the spirit of the building; but conversely, one old piece in a very modern hall can look stunning as can one very good new piece in an old entrance. Old or decoratively painted chests are always useful in halls. Desks (as tidy as possible) make the place look lived in. And very often the space under a staircase can make a useful study area or home office. A wall full of bookshelves is certainly welcoming. And if you have the luxury of a fireplace, nothing can be more welcoming in the winter or on a gloomy day, especially with a club fender, its brass beautifully polished, before it. Talking of which, it makes a great difference to a hall's welcoming appearance if any brass doorknobs or door furniture are kept well-polished, even if the paint work is somewhat less than spanking new. There is something about the look of obvious care that is comforting in itself.

Pairs of pedestals, plinths, urns, and busts, or oversized pots with flowering trees, look handsome either side of a door if there is the space; or just one pedestal and urn, indoor tree, bust, or piece of sculpture can look good in a corner. Decorative screens certainly provide interest in a hall and can be good draft-stoppers as well, in itself a comfort. And if you have a wide enough hall, you might be able to make the space an extra, if not permanent, dining area by adding a table that can hold books, plants, flowers, a tray of drinks, and so on when not in use for eating. Or in any event, try to fit in a side table or a console to hold the same sort of things.

However small the space though, an entrance hall can always be cheered with paintings, prints, framed photographs (getting to be such collectors' items now), sculpture, collections of this and that, and general memorabilia, as can staircase walls and landing areas. Once again, don't forget mirrors, even a collection of mirrors. They are the best way of making a space look larger than it is, and of adding sparkle and light. And if there is a window in the hall, a mirror will throw light back into the space. A small hall could be made to look very stylish with a series of silver or gilt *framed* panels of mirror (panels of mirror on their own can look very stark), set side by side about 12 inches (.3 m) apart on a painted background. Or the mirror panels can be covered with an ornamental, or not so ornamental, grille depending on the style of the space.

And finally, remember the sweet smells. A vase or vases of fragrant flowers or cache-pots of plants in season—freesias, narcissi, lilac, lilies, ginger blossoms, white wisteria hyacinths, gardenias, old-fashioned roses, sweet peas—all of them are delicious. Alternatives are bowls of potpourri changed or revitalized regularly, baskets of fresh lavender or bowls of dried lavender, and scented candles, fresh and flowery or citrus-like in hot weather, musky or spicy in cold.

I always keep small bottles of an essential oil such as lavender, and every so often sprinkle a few drops on the floor covering, or any fabric around so that there is a permanent gentle lavender smell in the house. This, of course, goes for any room except the kitchen.

*A vase of fresh flowers or potted plants add lovely fragrance, as will bowls of potpourri, baskets of dried flowers, and scented candles.*

# Yellow

TOP: *When planning a color scheme using warm yellows, think of the colors that harmonize with this shade, including various reds, rich browns, and dark leafy greens.*

ABOVE: *In small spaces like a hall or stairwell, combine deep yellow walls with grays, beiges, and browns, as in this wildlife print collection with polished wood frames.*

WARM YELLOWS are certainly in the same comfort range as reds and share many tones in common, such as coral and terra-cotta, shrimp and melon (cantaloupe or Cavaillon, not honeydew or Ogen). But then pale yellows can be as cooling in hot climates as lemon sherbet or sorbet. A real yellow-yellow is the color of sunlight, gold, sandy beaches, buttercups and dandelions in summer meadows, and fields full of ripening corn. It is equally the color of glowing fires, fall sunsets and turning leaves, and lighted windows at night. The color yellow is associated with brightness and cheerfulness, warmth and sparkle. It begins subtly, with palest blond hair, hay, honey, butter and sweet corn; swirls through lemons, daffodils, and jonquils; basks in the glow of peaches and apricots, melons, mangoes, papayas, mandarins, tangerines, and oranges; and ends with the glow of topaz and amber, the crunch of butterscotch and toffee, the spiciness of nutmeg, and the tawny depths of umber.

In nature, yellow is often found as a background color: a mellow ocher stone wall, a stretch of sand, a field of sunflowers. To plan a color scheme using warm yellows, think of such backgrounds, and the other colors that either contrast or harmonize with this shade will also come to mind. Think, for example, of the ripe corn complete with the odd patch of scorched earth, the splashes of scarlet created by clumps of poppies among the burnished gold, the edging of grass and trees.

Yellow, along with red and blue, is one of the three primary colors. Blue and red together produce purple, the complementary color to yellow; therefore, all shades of purple—from pale lilac, lavender, and mauve through to iris, amethyst, and eggplant—will go well with yellow. So will very pale as well as dark and olive greens; dashes of different blues; and various reds, from terra-cotta to rose madder and Venetian red or ox-blood. Warm yellows also look good with tones of ivory, beige, biscuit, stone, and ecru.

In a large space try sponged, rubbed, or dragged egg yolk yellow walls with white trim and ecru ceiling; coir matting; touches of black, purply blue, dark red, and green; and some blue and white porcelain. In a smaller space deeper or more muted yellow walls can be used with lavenders, pale blue-greens, blue-grays, silver grays, and browns, as in polished wood furniture or floorboards. If you think of using any sort of apricot, melon, shrimp, peach, or yellowed coral colors, avoid solid paint. It is much better to drag or stipple, rag rub or glaze to build up to the required tone. Any of these colors will then go with anything: rose tones, creams, off-white, white, stone, blues, greens, browns, or grays.

Like red and orange, yellows are advancing colors, bringing surfaces apparently closer to the eye. But a word of caution: Yellow and orange lie next to each other on the color wheel and should not be used in equal quantities in a space or they will cancel each other out. Nor will equal quantities of red and yellow be particularly restful with no other leavening. If you think that a mixture of yellow and red paint in smaller or larger quantities and lightened, as necessary, by white will produce a perfectly satisfactory apricot to orange range, think again. As Annie Sloan and Kate Gwynn say in their book *Color in Decoration* (Little, Brown, 1990), the apricots mixed from this tend to look too sickly and the oranges too hot and harsh. Far better, they suggest, to start with an earthier base such as burnt sienna or a light red. Then add a touch of cadmium yellow, or yellow ocher to achieve a warm orange. To this mixture, add white as needed to soften down to a range of tones from apricot to melon. Orange tones need cool contrasts: cool greens and blues, real lime green (not that synthetic-looking color commonly known as lime), and white. And, for particular warmth in a gray climate, use burnt orange or cantaloupe with umber, nutmeg, chocolate brown, and hues of gray (as in flagstones) with perhaps a strong dash of white.

Finally, a lively scheme that would be appropriate in any climate can be worked around a honeysuckle flower. Think how the yellow dissolves into a rich cream with tinges of rose and apricot and organize wall, floor, window treatments, and accessories accordingly.

GLAZED RIPE CORN OR SAFFRON WALLS; COIR AND SISAL MATTING, HONEY-COLORED FLOORBOARDS, OR DEEP GREEN AND ECRU TILES; GOLDEN AFGHAN RUGS; YELLOW AND RED PRINTED FABRICS; OLD STONE AND LACQUERED INDIAN RED ALL LOOK GOOD TOGETHER.

*Burnt orange walls accented with floors, furniture, and accessories in various shades of brown, and cream or off-white moldings, make a warm and welcoming setting in any climate.*

# LIVING ROOMS AND FAMILY ROOMS
# Rooms for One and All

*The sentiment of having a leisurely evening at home after a hectic day is more or less universal. So is the desire for real comfort and the means for relaxation in the room in which we sit or put up our feet, whether it is the living room, family room, or den.*

We expect a good deal from the rooms in which we spend our waking leisure hours, for whether they be living rooms, family rooms, or a mixture of both, we have to accommodate our own needs as well as those of each member of the family and visiting friends. Unless you are fortunate enough to possess a more formal drawing room or a den more or less set aside for adults as well as a more casual family room, or a library, or play space, the living room is not only the designated room for conversation, looking at television, listening to music, reading, playing cards, and—if there is no other space—for children's play, it is also the room that is most on show, as it were, both as a family room and as an entertaining room.

Whatever the nomenclature, the vital thing is that any one of these leisure rooms—which I shall call the general grouping—should be more of a *personal* room than a room for show. (You could perhaps make an exception of a formal drawing room, although that too, while not necessarily needing to be so multifunctional, should definitely emphasize a general level of comfort.) Depending on size, leisure-time rooms should contain not only really comfortable and well-arranged seating, but the furniture, rugs, objects, and art that you are really happy with—things that mean something to you: family heirlooms, proud flea market finds, pieces you have found and painted and personalized yourself, pieces that are sentimental to you for one reason and another. They should be pieces that you have chosen because you liked them so much, all the things in fact that you find comforting and with which you want to be surrounded. And if the living room is the only space in the home where children can play, then at least make sure that there are cupboards, chests, baskets—even a table with a long tablecloth will do—in or under which you can stuff the playthings when it's time to give over the space to the grown-ups.

OPPOSITE: *Living rooms should contain really comfortable and well-arranged seating, with objects and art that are sentimental and meaningful to you. Deeply cushioned sofas, lots of fluffy throw pillows, and family heirlooms make a room that is comforting and personal.*

BELOW: *When accessorizing your living room, surround yourself with the things you most desire. Vases of fragrant flowers, stacks of much-loved books, and leisure-time diversions, like board games, puzzles, or needlework, are just right in this leisure time room.*

# Creating a Relaxing Leisure-Time Room

TOP: *Light from table lamps, up-lights, and wall lights can bounce attractively from well-placed mirrors. If your general light is from table lamps, however, be sure that the light can be turned on or off by a switch by the door.*

ABOVE: *If you are able to decide ahead of time where outlets and fixtures will be placed, you will be able to avoid a messy tangle of wires. This is especially true in rooms such as this one, where there is little chance of concealing electrical wires and cords.*

## LIGHTING

First for comfort in living rooms, family rooms, and dens is the lighting and temperature, rather than the furniture and its arrangement. First on two counts: one, because, as I stress, if you are designing a room from scratch, you need to get all the wiring (and any insulation and pipe work for heating) done before any decoration is started. Two, because a comfortable level of light, and air control that can be modulated successfully for any activity or occasion, has to be planned with careful forethought. Even if you are trying to make an existing, and sometimes ancient, room more comfortable, you will still need to work out what possible changes or additions you can make without wrecking the status quo.

If you are able to plan your lighting from the start—to decide where each outlet should be placed, to which point each light should be directed, and which fixture or lamp will produce the most appropriate kind of light—you will not only be very lucky, you will also be able to avoid the tangle of wires and cords that beset most rooms whose owners have tried to produce as good as possible lighting without changing the existing wiring plan. The end result might be considerably better than before, but it will always be a compromise.

In any event, it will be extremely useful to draw up a room plan with the furniture arrangement worked out (see pages 48–57). This way you can also work out what light to use where, where you can put unencumbered heat outlets, and the least conspicuous places to put thermostats and, in apartments, call boxes. It is extraordinary how often these items are invariably placed exactly where you want to place a sofa, or on a wall, where they are either glaringly obvious or where they prevent you from hanging any paintings or prints.

### BACKGROUND LIGHTING

All leisure-time rooms need reasonable ambient or general light. Such light is achieved by ceiling fixtures of one sort or another—from the ubiquitous center light, to recessed spots, to a whole illuminated ceiling; lights concealed behind valances or cornices; wall lights, up-lights, and table lamps. If you are against ceiling light (with the exception of recessed spots for highlighting art and objects), or have old or ornamental ceilings you do not want to disturb, or too-shallow ceiling recesses, or concrete ceilings that obviate recessed lighting, do not worry. Table lamps, well-placed up-lights (in corners, behind sofas, and in large plants), or wall lights can all bounce light off from ceilings or walls and are perfectly good alternatives to ceiling fixtures.

I myself am against central ceiling fixtures in any sort of living room for the simple reason that the best artificial light is meant to emulate the many moods of daylight. And since the sun does not stand still in the middle of the sky all day long, why should we go on trying to reproduce perpetual midday sun? This is exactly what we do with an unsubtle central light. The exception to this is an elegant chandelier in a formal drawing room, or one of the newly fashionable, very pretty and intricate chandeliers in a living room, as long as it is attached to a dimmer switch. Of course, if a formal room is large enough to take two or three chandeliers then that is both grand and effective.

If you decide to achieve your general or ambient light with lamps or up-lights, however, do try to ensure that you have the ability to switch at least one or two and preferably all lights on and off from the door. It is irritating to have to crawl around to switch off up-lights (concealed behind plants or large pieces of furniture or in corners) at baseboard level, and a relief not to have to go around and switch on or off each table lamp in turn. This is unavoidable unless you have had, or can have, a secondary 5-amp circuit installed without too much fuss and bother, which makes switching from the doorway possible.

*It is a good idea to work out the furniture and lighting arrangement ahead of time. If the room is large enough to take two or three ceiling lights attached to dimmer switches, as well as several table lamps, the effect can be quite warm and comforting.*

TOP: *Floor lamps should measure about 40 to 49 inches to the lower edge of the shade. If the lamp is taller, it should be placed behind your shoulder for reading. Bear in mind that for needlework, you will need much higher bulb wattage.*

ABOVE: *Lamps look best with an open-top shade in a moderately translucent material such as paper, cotton, or silk. Large lamps like those pictured look well with slightly tapered shades, while more steeply tapered shades are best on small, spindly lamps.*

# Choosing the Right Lamp

When you are shopping for leisure room lamps, keep the following in mind.

- The total height from the floor to the lower edge of the shade (including table height) should equal the average eye height from the floor (for example, 38 to 42 inches/97 to 107 cm) when seated in an easy chair.

- Choose three-way (50/100/150-watt or 100/200/300-watt) or regular soft-white bulbs (150/200-watt) for reading (so they can be dimmed when not needed to light a page). If a lamp has two sockets, put in one bright white bulb for reading and one low-wattage pink bulb for a gentler atmosphere. Brass, chrome, or nickel adjustable floor lamps look good, but remember that they are very seldom capable of taking more than a 60-watt bulb, and mostly only take 40-watt. Still, they work well enough for the clear-sighted. The base height of floor lamps should be 40 to 49 inches (102 to 124 cm) to the lower edge of the shade. If for some reason the shade is substantially above eye level, the lamp should be placed behind your shoulder for reading. If this is not possible (if, for example, a chair or sofa is against a wall, or the room is small and the furniture is close to walls and windows), use swing-arm wall lamps with 100- to 150-watt bulbs or floor lamps with adjustable spots and dimmer attachments.

- An open-top shade on a lamp is best, with a minimum bottom dimension of 16 inches (41 cm). Shallower shades need a louver or shield on top. Almost all lampshades look better slightly tapered, with vertical measurements a little larger than the top diameter. More steeply tapered shades with a much smaller top than bottom diameter look best on small, rather spindly lamps and should be small in proportion. For reading—and actually for general aesthetics—it is better to have moderately translucent material such as translucent paper, linen, cotton and silk, parchment laminated to fabric, or, if the fabric is dense, a white or rose lining. Some designers always use subtle rose-colored linings on shades or at least rose-colored bulbs for the warmer and more atmospheric light that this gives, although here again it is a gentle fight between aesthetics and practicality. Only use dense or opaque shades if the walls are dark, and keep in mind that all shades in a room should be similar in brightness but not dead white, which causes glare.

- Work lamps are usually best at 15 inches (38 cm) high to the lower edge of the shade—or about eye level for the average adult. If they are for writing it is best if they are placed 15 inches (38 cm) to the left of a work center (or to the right for a left-handed person) and 12 inches (30 cm) back from the front edge of a desk or work table. The shade should be light and open at the top, with a white or near-white lining; the ideal bulb is a soft white 200-watt or a 50/200/250 three-way.

- For swing-arm desk lamps, swing the shade closer to the front edge of the desk.

- If you want light for sewing, embroidery, or tapestry work—which many people find remarkably soothing—you really need twice as much light as for casual reading, so bulb wattage must be as high as possible.

The most comfortable lighting for any room that is primarily for relaxing is a mixture of background light generated by up-lights and/or concealed light, localized light cast by lamps, and decorative accent lighting. And all of it should be capable of being dimmed, whether by dimmer switches or three-way switches, to whatever level of light is preferred at any one time according to need and mood.

### LIGHTING FOR READING AND CLOSE WORK

In addition to general background lighting, you should also ensure that there is good reading light for everyone who wants it, which means lamps by certain designated sofas and chairs. (*Not,* please note, every chair, or the room will look like a denuded forest.) Another priority is a good work light if you need to write or do close work of any kind (such as needlework, tapestry, or any other hobby that requires clear illumination).

### LIGHTING FOR ART AND OBJECTS

I have mentioned the importance of *variety* in lighting in leisure-time rooms, and accent lighting, however it is produced, will provide just such a change in lighting levels. Depending on what objects or areas you would like to highlight, you will need specific types of lights.

## Comfort Zoning
### LIGHTBULB BASICS

Remember that a truly comfortable reading and work light means that the bulb wattage should be capable of being as high as possible. Make sure that the light fitting you choose can take a higher wattage than 60-watt. A surprising number don't.

*Lighting art and objects is best done with a variety of light sources. Objects on shelves and tables can be picked out with tiny spots. Framing projectors, as well as down-lights or spots mounted on a track or wire, can be used to light individual wall hangings, paintings, or sculpture.*

- **Bookshelves** look dramatic when lit from the sides by strip lights concealed behind baffles, or from the top by lighting hidden behind a valance of some kind, or by wall washers inset into the ceiling. The trick is to make sure that light grazes the book spines all the way down the shelves.

- **Objects on shelves** can be picked out by tiny portable spots. Collections of glass, ceramics, and other small objects look particularly arresting in front of a translucent wall (made by fixing vertical strip lights to the wall behind a set of shelves and concealing them with panels of white plexiglass, acrylic, or obscured glass). Glass-fronted cabinets can be lit with rows of tiny bulbs inset into Plugmold or a miniature track installed either along the front edge of each shelf or vertically down the sides of the cabinet. In either case the lights should be concealed behind slim baffles. The same sort of method can be used to light alcoves with shelves used for display. If a single object is to be displayed in an alcove, it might be possible to light it by a miniature recessed light fixed into the ceiling of the alcove.

- **A whole wall of pictures, prints, drawings, photographs, wall hangings, or whatever** can be satisfactorily lit by using recessed wall washers set back about 3 feet to 3 feet 6 inches (.9 to 1.06 m) from the wall, which will literally wash the whole area with light. The advantage of this type of lighting is that individual pieces can be moved around or changed without having to readjust the lights. The disadvantage is that you will need to be prepared for a lack of contrast between the pictures and the surrounding wall and a lessening of any textural qualities that a painting might have.

- **Individual paintings, pieces of sculpture, or other works of art** can best be lit with a framing projector, which with its use of lenses and a shutter will allow the beam of light to fall only upon the painting. Its control can be very finely adjusted, usually to within a quarter inch or so. Another method is to use down-lights or spots either mounted on a track or wire or recessed into the ceiling. One advantage in using a track or stretched wire is the ease with which the amount of light on a painting is controlled, not only by a dimmer switch but also by means of different housings and wattages of bulbs that are adjustable and can also light individual paintings and objects. Another advantage is the evenness of light that it is possible to project. The disadvantages are the amount of hardware that is evident; the fact that the beam from an ordinary down-light will form an elliptical shape on the wall so that it will be lighting parts of the wall as well as the painting itself; and the inability of closely controlling the beam of a spotlight versus the beam from a framing projector. It is a good idea to get catalogs from lightbulb or fixture manufacturers to find out the wattage and beam spread needed for your own specific picture sizes as well as how far away the paintings and objects should be from the light source for maximum results.

ABOVE: *Collections of small objects or framed photographs can be highlighted with subtle accent lighting. Be sure to find the best possible angle to show the display to its best advantage.*

OPPOSITE: *Walls with generous displays of pictures and prints can be nicely lit using recessed wall washers, which bathe the entire wall in light. This method of lighting will allow you to move individual pieces around without having to readjust the lights.*

TOP: *Experiment with lighting objects from different levels and angles. While a change in light direction may have little effect on some objects, it can make a great difference on others, especially intricate sculptures and reliefs.*

ABOVE: *Light fixtures are often decorative and an integral part of a tabletop display. Decorative accent lights, like this lamp, should be capable of being dimmed to whatever level is comfortable according to your mood and time of day.*

- **If you cannot recess lights into the ceiling** for one reason or another, dislike holes in ceilings or any form of stretched wire or track lighting, or are in a rental or an old house where you think such lights might be obtrusive, you could try lighting from below with up-lights or small spots (such as T10 25-, 40-, or 60-watt, or R20 50-watt reflector bulbs) concealed in urns or planters, on mantels or similar horizontal surfaces, or behind a sofa if it stands far enough away from the wall (but not if there will be foot traffic between the sofa and the wall).

- **Alternatively, you can use conventional picture lights** mounted on the painting to light it from above, with a rotating reflector, adjustable from the wall to adapt to an extra-thick picture frame. The length of the reflector should be one-third to one-half the width of the painting. Use tubular 25- to 40-watt bulbs on 9-inch (23-cm) centers. The disadvantages are that unless you have an electric outlet just behind the painting, you will have an unsightly cord showing, and in any event, the light on top of the painting will be much brighter than the light at the bottom.

- **Plants, floor-standing sculpture, and wall hangings** can be lit by up-lights concealed behind plants, positioned in corners, or placed beside the object to be lit. The up-lights will either bounce light up or graze the given object with light. Alternatively, you can use small adjustable floor spotlights. Again, try to have all these lights on a dimmer switch, preferably controlled near the door or at least at an accessible level on the wall.

It is irritating in any sort of room that is meant to be relaxing to find art and objects that are *overlit*, that is to say, both too brightly and with too much overspill for the general comfort level. Accent light should be as subtle as it is accurate in highlighting what you most want to show.

When using accent lighting, it is not enough to use the correct type of light. It is also important to find the best possible angle to light the painting or object to its best advantage.

Buy or borrow an inexpensive work light used by contractors to light their work, and experiment with different angles to see what gives the best effect. With some paintings the direction of light makes very little difference, but others may have enough varnish on the surface to cause light from certain angles either to glance back uncomfortably into somebody's eyes or to distort the painting—sometimes to the extent of making the contents disappear altogether.

Theoretically, lighting fixtures should be placed so that light hits the center of a painting at an angle of 30 degrees from the vertical. This should prevent reflections from the frame, glass, or surface of the picture, and also avoids shadows from the frame or especially thick paint texture and so on. However, for various practical reasons, you might not be able to use that angle because of the shape of the room or the position in which the painting has had to be hung. And you should certainly check the normal sight lines of people seated or standing in the room to ensure that no uncomfortable unshielded light sources are in view.

One interesting point to remember is that artists usually paint by daylight indoors and tend to favor painting by the light of a north window because north light does not change color as much as light from other parts of the sky (in the southern hemisphere of course, painters pick a south window). This light is bluer than the incandescent variety normally found in most people's homes, and some museums and art galleries use extremely pale blue filters over incandescent bulbs to eliminate the yellowness and to approximate as closely as possible the light the painter was working with in the first place. This is certainly worth experimenting with at home as well.

Do not forget too that if the major surfaces of a room are at all strongly colored, some of the color will be reflected onto the painting or paintings as well. And make sure that there isn't an excessive difference between the lighted painting(s) and the surrounding areas. Also, a very high level of illumination over a long period of time might cause deterioration to the paint surface.

*An elegant chandelier in a formal living room can look grand while offering a reasonable amount of general lighting. Supplement the ceiling fixture with well-placed table lamps and wall lights.*

## WINDOWS

Windows are as much a part of the background of a room as the walls, and are immediately noticeable elements; so the way you treat them makes an enormous difference to the character of the space. Neat, architectural-looking shutters, for example, or spare Roman shades, or other crisp-looking blinds will make a room seem very "of the moment," even if it is more than half full of antique furniture. Curtains in the same room, or, say, Austrian shades will make the ambiance much more traditional.

But comfort, as I keep remarking, is a compendium of all sorts of things. Items must work with ease too. Warped or badly installed shutters that don't quite close or whose louvers do not work too well and sloppily drawn-up Roman shades or other types of blinds destroy the harmony of a room. (Note that it is possible to have Roman shades made with heavy enough rods in the back and sturdy enough cords to prevent this all-too-common carelessness.) Equally, curtains must be well-made and of appropriate style for both the window and the room. Very elaborate curtains in a perfectly normal modern room with no particular architectural details can look absurdly pretentious.

*Curtains should be in a style that is appropriate to both the windows and room. Elegant curtains such as these would look incongruous in a thoroughly modern setting. Use a generous amount of fabric for a luxurious look.*

## CURTAINS

Curtains were originally developed to keep out drafts and outside weather conditions and for privacy as well as for their decorative looks. And although central heating, insulation, and products such as Thermopane are supposed to deal with the outside cold and air conditioning with the outside heat, the fact remains that with the best will in the world, not everyone has the best heating and air-conditioning systems, and, more often than one might suspect, they have neither. Nor are many old houses possible to insulate altogether successfully, and it is here that curtains really come into their own as far as physical comfort is concerned.

Properly lined and interlined curtains made from a heavy fabric will make a fabulous difference to a drafty old window, especially if there are also shades to let down behind them. Or if you want a crisper look that is also a draft-saver, you can use some sort of shade with curtains permanently drawn back at either sides both to counteract the effects of ill-fitting old frames and to provide a softening of line.

## SHUTTERS

All old southern European houses and very many American ones have outside shutters, and for a very good reason. Drawn shutters during the day are a defense against the intrusive sun and keep the (mainly) non–air-conditioned rooms shadowy and cool.

Since almost all windows in southern Europe open inward while most American and Antipodean windows are of the sash variety, and since most shutters have some sort of decorative air holes if they are solid, or louvers if they are not, there is still plenty of air circulation.

## COLORS

Clearly, if a room's main role is to provide relaxation outside the bedroom and bathroom, its color scheme should be easy on the eye. You need to choose colors that will nurture not dazzle, comfort not distract. But as always, of course, the kind of color scheme you decide on should depend on geographical location, climate, aspect, and style of home, quite apart from personal taste, existing furnishings and possessions, family needs, and lifestyle. All of these factors need to be taken into consideration.

For real comfort what you should try to achieve is a welcoming background, a certain comforting serenity—feeling that is often provided by subtle and unexpected variations of tones and neutrals: the soft grays and beiges or gray-greens and khakis with various whites; the nutmegs and nut colors and russets with tobaccos and coffees and soft creams; the ivories and soft apricots and pale marmalades; the soft, deep, slightly yellowy roses and so on. Rarely however, at least in a family living room or den that is much-used, can you employ the really delicate pale pastels and mainly whites, or creams with blues and greens. These colors will either look gracelessly grubby in no time, or make one terrified of spoiling the unruffled calm in any way and therefore tense and unrelaxed.

## Comfort Zoning
**CURTAIN BASICS**

Curtains will look far better if you use a generous amount of a simple, reasonably priced fabric rather than a skimpy amount of a very expensive one. And don't even think of designing elaborate curtains for a nondescript room. It would be far better to spend the money on adding some simple architectural detailing.

THE KIND OF COLOR SCHEME YOU DECIDE ON SHOULD DEPEND UPON GEOGRAPHICAL LOCATION, CLIMATE, ASPECT, AND STYLE OF HOME, QUITE APART FROM PERSONAL TASTE, EXISTING FURNISHINGS, FAMILY NEEDS, AND LIFESTYLE.

SURELY THERE CAN BE
NO DOUBT THAT THE
IDEAL PLACE FOR ANY
RELAXING, READING,
OR CONVERSATIONAL
AREA IS AROUND
HAPPILY CRACKLING,
FLICKERING, AND OFTEN
MESMERIZING FLAMES.

*I cannot imagine a comfortable leisure-time room without a fireplace, especially in any location that has cool or gloomy weather. Sitting around a radiator or warm-air duct is just not as appealing.*

## WALLS

The only way, I suppose, to make walls in any way tactile and comfortable to the touch is to cover them with a suitable fabric. This process will cover up faults in the plastering (as long as there is no damp) and make the room better insulated and more soundproof. (While many people find fabric walls very comfortable and luxurious, others sometimes find them claustrophobic or think they should be used only in bedrooms.)

If you would like a "touchable" wall, there are several ways of doing this:

1  Get fabric paper-backed, which various wall specialists will do, and paste it up like wallpaper.

2  Paste a firm fabric straight onto the walls (pasting the walls, not the fabric).

3  Clip the stretched and stitched panels of fabric to lengths of metal made just for that purpose, fixed just under the ceiling and just above the baseboards. Or gather it onto rods fixed under ceilings and above baseboards.

4  Let lengths of seamed fabric hang loose from rods fixed just below the ceiling level.

5  Make padded walls, or "walling," which is a technique very popular in France. This is the traditional way of putting fabric on walls and involves laying some sort of interlining or wadding (known in the trade as "bump") between slim wood battens nailed to the walls at regular intervals. Fabric is then sewn together in panels and stapled to the top and bottom of the walls below any cornice or cove and above baseboards. Strips of braid, or piping, or thin strips of gilded or silvered wood hide the staples. If a patterned fabric is used, it does, of course, have to be carefully matched.

## FIREPLACES

Perhaps nothing suggests the comfort and coziness of a leisure room as a fireplace and a brightly burning fire within it. Although I realize that it is not always possible to have a fireplace, I personally cannot conceive of a comfortable leisure-time room without one, at least in any country that has semblance of winter and gloomy wet days or nights. I feel this so viscerally that I cannot imagine moving into a home that lacks this, to me, essential ingredient, or at least a home without the possibility of installing one. Nor, for that matter, could I possibly write a book dealing with comfort in the home without going into the whole subject of fireplaces. If any reader does not possess a fireplace, and does not yearn for one, then this section should be skipped.

All through the history of the house, the fireplace has provided the focal point, the essence, one could say, of the comforting sense of home quite apart from much of a room's architectural character. Nor is it by accident that the two words "hearth" and "home" are so often linked together emotively. Not only do they share the same word in some languages (the French *foyer* derived from the

Latin *focarium* (m), *focus* (f) can mean both "hearth" and "home" as can the Swedish *hem*), but the fireplace has traditionally and literally provided both the focal point of a room as well as its warmth and glow and, with the help of rush lights, candles, or oil lamps, its light. Up until the twentieth century, almost every house in any cold-climate country would have a fireplace.

The general advent of the central heating boiler and the sentiment of "Out with the old, in with the new" in the past century contributed to the fireplace's demise, at least for a time. But sitting around a radiator or a warm-air duct hardly provides the same allure as sitting around a blazing fire; nor is it easy to find as good a focal point as a fireplace to furnish a room around. The result is that many developers are once again providing fireplaces as a matter of course, however efficient the heating system.

Happily, with prefabricated double-walled and lined flues, which can be well-insulated and threaded through the building to reappear at roof level, it is now comparatively easy to replace or install fireplaces in any room in any house. It is not quite so easy in apartment buildings, of course, unless an apartment is on the top floor. Moreover, as the British architect Nicholas Hills points out in his most

*Fireplaces often provide the focal point of the room, as well as its warmth, glow, and need I say, comfort. And it can define and enhance the architectural character of a room, as seen in this fireplace with its magnificent carved mantle.*

# Comforting Woods

City and town dwellers have got used to buying whatever anonymous wood they can for their fires in plastic sacks from supermarkets, hardware stores, and filling stations. But in the old days one bought, or went out and collected, both particularly aromatic woods and wood for specific purposes. If you do have a selection of woods to choose from, here are some wood types and characteristics to keep in mind.

- **Ash** has always been a great favorite, wet or dry, for its clear, strong flame. As the old saying goes, "Burn ashwood green, 'tis fit for a queen," which is why, of course, so many early communities planted ash groves next to their villages and towns.
- **Cherry and Apple** have a particularly sweet smell when burning.
- **Cypress** has a more aromatic scent.
- **Hawthorn and Hornbeam** burn almost as well as ash.
- **Chestnut, Beech, and Oak,** the denser hardwood timbers, burn better—and last much longer—for being well-seasoned, that is to say, kept for at least a year after felling. **Beech** was used for baking bread (many old fireplaces incorporate bread ovens) because it burns with such an even heat.
- **Pine, Spruce, and other softwoods** light quickly but generally burn too quickly and throw a lot of sparks, although they are good for starting fires.
- **Juniper** was used for smoking and curing hams.
- **Australian Ironwood,** available in the Antipodes, burns long and satisfactorily, once it gets going.
- **Peat,** if you can get it (and it has been compressed to form convenient blocks), though not a wood since it is made from dried bits of mossy bog land, burns rapidly but then smolders for a long time. This makes it ideal for keeping an open fire overnight; and used judiciously with other fuel, it can help modulate a fire's combustion. It was, of course, the traditional fuel of Ireland.
- **Kindling** can be literally any sort of wood in the form of twigs or small branches, or split into thin sticks.

LEFT: *New fireplaces can be creatively sited, such as between rooms or on a window wall. The chimney can be used as a sculptural element or display area, with the mantel flush or shallow against the wall.*

OPPOSITE: *Just as fresh flowers are so important in lending fragrance and ambience throughout the home, aromatic woods will burn and fill your home with delightful and comforting scents.*

informative *The English Fireplace* (Quiller Press Ltd., 1983), new fireplaces can be sited in more imaginative places: between windows, for example, or on a window wall, so that people sitting around the fireside can get a good view of the outside—if it is worth viewing. If the flue can be rather abruptly angled sideways in the wall, a fireplace can be installed with a window above, or a modern fireplace can be positioned in the center of a wall of glass or windows, with the flue used as a sculptural element against the transparency of the glass. In a new house, a sculptural-looking chimney can be installed between two rooms—a living room and dining room say, or a dining room and kitchen—to provide a fireplace on both sides as well as a handsome dividing feature. In this way the fireplace, particularly between a dining room and kitchen, can act as an indoor barbecue too—a modern version of its old "spit and roast" use.

Much the same sort of effect can be achieved in older houses with small rooms and back-to-back fireplaces. Most of the dividing wall can be dismantled to make one much larger room, leaving the chimney stack (which is often decorative in its own right) intact. It is often well worth the trouble of stripping off the existing plaster to reveal the interesting brickwork underneath, which can then be cleaned down (or replastered if not in such good condition). Depending on the heights of the two fireplaces and the air currents circulating around the room, it is sometimes possible to combine the two openings into one, and thus the fireplace will be open on both sides. This usually requires a good deal of experimentation to make sure that the single flame draws efficiently; and almost certainly the throat

## Comfort Zoning
### FIRE LOG BASICS

It is best to replenish stocks of logs during the summer months. They will be less expensive then, and certainly will burn better for the keeping. Logs for the average fireplace should be about 1 foot long (.3 m). Larger ones, of course, are good for larger fireplaces, especially as they burn for much longer. For this reason, larger logs are useful for putting on last thing at night to keep a fire burning.

TOP: *When the fireplace is not in use, fill the space with neat stacks of logs or baskets of flowers or greenery.*

ABOVE: *While gas logs or coal fires can be easily inserted into old fireplaces, nothing equals the smell of aromatic wood smoke.*

OPPOSITE: *Centuries ago, gentlemen would meet at inns and gather on benches around the fireplace for relaxing conversation. Eventually, these inns became "clubs" and the fireplace hearth benches became known as "club fenders." Today club fenders still offer a warm spot to sit and enjoy the fire.*

at the base of the chimney will need to be reconstructed in order to make the upward draft; but the visual effect is well worth the trouble in the long run. Also, this will be more practical in a country house rather than a town one, because it will generally be more effective to burn large logs.

## THE COMFORT FACTOR OF FIREPLACES

While it may not be very comfortable to have to haul baskets of firewood or coal around and to clean up the ashes in the grate, there is something very homey about seeing neat stacks of logs by houses all ready for the heaving. And the appurtenances and ritual of fire-making (although not necessarily fire cleaning-up) may be seen as part of a homely ritual that includes the pervading winter smell of sweet wood smoke. Certainly, there is something about approaching a house on a cold, crisp day, seeing wisps of smoke curling out of the chimney, and smelling that comforting scent of burning wood in the air all around that really cannot be replicated by the vastly more convenient gas log or coal fires that can now be inserted very easily into old fireplaces. (On the other hand, wood-burning stoves that burn much more slowly and efficiently, and require much less attention, provide another, perhaps more practical but less romantic alternative, along with the nostalgic smells.)

## STOVES

We are, however, talking general creature comforts here as well as visual and emotional ones. It has to be admitted that with an open fire, more heat is lost to the outside air via the flue than in a closed stove, where combustion is controlled and the heat can be retained. The majority of closed stoves have a 70 percent efficiency rate compared with the 30 percent rate of an open fire. This fact, while not important in an efficient, centrally heated house where a fireplace is used more for its looks and focus than for heat, becomes more important when a fireplace is the sole heat source.

Perhaps, one of the best compromises is the Jetmaster Universal Grate, which is available in five different widths together with a range of special fittings so that it can be adapted to fit into a variety of existing old fireplaces. The Jetmaster is designed to allow air to circulate around the casing, creating a convection movement of warmed air around the room. Either coal or wood can be burned by inserting different burner trays, and the fire can also be fitted with a water heater based on a hermetically sealed heat pipe system. Another compromise, particularly used in France, is to have a fireplace with its own let-down glass front that can then be slid back underneath the fire when you want it to look like a regular open fire. A close-fitting ash pan is installed underneath the grate with adjustable air controls like a closed stove, which provides a measured amount of ventilation to the fire, as well as regulating the temperature of air underneath the fire. When

you go out, or to bed, you can shut both the air control and the glass front, and the fire, with luck, will keep burning for many hours, much as in a closed stove.

The Norwegians too, makers of the well-known Jotul stove, produce a generously sized grate that can fit into an existing fireplace or into a corner and that can also be fitted with a back boiler. It has the advantages of a stove with its own doors, which, left open, give it the appearance of an open fire. And it has a facility for drawing cold air either from the room or directly from outside which then circulates around the back of the casing before issuing into the room. This means that there is a constant renewal of fresh (but not cold) air.

Of course, over the centuries the Scandinavians have also perfected the handsome ceramic stoves that are covetable in their own right, as are many of the old (and new) cast iron and polished steel American stoves made in Vermont and Maine. Vermont Castings makes other justifiably popular stoves, which again can be used as open fires or as air-tight heaters.

## FLOORING

There are hard floor lovers, close-carpeted floor lovers, and those that compromise with wood, marble, limestone, or tiled floors topped by a large area rug or one or two or more smaller rugs. This is a good solution for those who might like the occasional dance surface after dinner or for a party, or who like the option of being able to take up all the rugs to leave a clean, cool, uncluttered surface for hot summer months.

## Comfort Zoning
### RUG AND CARPET BACKING BASICS

If rugs are going to be part of your room's décor, remember to use a sticky underlay, cut to measure, underneath them to obviate hazardous slipping. Again, use a sticky backing underneath to prevent any rug from riding up and wrinkling. And while we are on the subject of backing, a good underlay will not only extend the life of a carpet or floor covering but will make it a great deal more comfortable, which, after all, is the object of the exercise.

If you are designing a room from scratch and want a combination of wood or tile and a large area rug or carpet, it is a good and practical idea to buy the rug or carpet first, tape around the floor area you want to cover with it, and then have the wood or tile laid all around, leaving an inset for the soft flooring. This may sound miserly but it's actually very practical, because there will be no danger of slippage and there is little point, after all, in covering an expensive hard floor with a large area of rug. In a hot climate where both staying cool and having your rooms *look* cool is the ultimate comfort, you could do much the same thing with cool white or cream tile (ceramic, limestone, marble, or travertine), using one or the other of them as the "rug."

If carpet is the choice, one of the most elegant weaves to choose for a living room that does not get an excessive amount of traffic is a plush finish. This texture is achieved by cutting all the loops of the wool, synthetic fibers, or mixture in the weave to the same height. This type of finish does not have the resilience or the resistance to dirt given by a tightly woven loop quality, which is more useful for high-traffic areas, but it does provide both elegance and a comfortable look quite apart from its comfort underfoot. Another elegant surface, but slightly fragile if you have dogs and cats with claws, is Brussels Weave, which looks like an immaculate, oversize piece of cross-stitch wool work. Of course, nowadays too there are all sorts of mixed-weave carpets, with some areas that are plush or tightly woven and others that are shaggier, to form an interesting self-colored pattern or design.

Another popular choice is coir or sisal or sea grass woven matting, or (particularly in rural houses) woven rush matting, or, rather more luxurious, wool or wool mixture versions of the same. These are great unifiers of different kinds of furniture and make even a traditional room look updated. And like hard floors (or carpets too, for that matter), these can take a rug or two or three on top. With their edges nicely bound in a contrast tape or material, they make handsome rugs on a hard floor themselves.

ABOVE: *A comfy sofa with soft, loose cushions is perfect for relaxing. When selecting fabric furnishings and flooring, consider your lifestyle and needs—and whether the room will be used by children and/or pets.*

OPPOSITE: *Top hardwood floors with one large area rug or several rugs in keeping with the overall decorating scheme. And always use a sticky underlay under a rug to prevent the rug from slipping and wrinkling.*

## A New Life for Worn or Torn Oriental Rugs

You can recycle battered old Oriental rugs by turning them into outside floor pillows for lounging around on. Try to find an unworn area about 3 or 4 feet by 6 feet (.9 or 1 m by 2 m). Cut out this piece and fold it in half with the back of the rug on the outside. Now take a heavy-duty carpet needle and heavy thread and stitch the sides of the remnant together. When that is accomplished, turn it inside out so that the carpet surface is now on the outside. Fill the resulting pouch with foam pellets until the pillow is nicely squashy, and sew up the opening. If you don't already possess a battered old rug or two, you can nearly always find them priced inexpensively at a garage sale.

# Room Arrangements

Since the ideal leisure-time room is one in which not only the family but visitors can feel relaxed and at home, and since, at least for families, it is a room that should work on many levels for different age groups as well as different interests, it follows that as much care should be taken with the *arrangement* of furniture, art, and accessories as with the choice of the individual pieces. Moreover, the room should *look* comfortable and welcoming even before that comfort is experienced physically.

It is easy to forget however, that making firm arrangements of furniture that are only slightly flexible (the ability to move around occasional chairs, ottomans, and footstools to expand and contract seating groups) is an essentially twentieth-century innovation. Before that, most of the pieces were lifted from the sides of the room where they were usually parked and moved around a great deal, particularly into one large conversational circle. Hence the French word *meubles* or "movables," for furniture, though admittedly that stemmed originally from the fact that in medieval times in Europe, the best pieces of furniture were moved from property to property as well. Then too, most affluent households had several servants to perform these duties. And if they were not affluent, they had very few pieces to move around anyway.

*Furniture arrangements should be planned ahead of time, with an eye to function and traffic pattern. Coffee tables should be set at a comfortable distance from sofas and chairs, with adequate space available for people to walk through the room.*

# FLOOR PLANS

Whether you are trying to make an existing room more comfortable, or are planning a whole new room that you want to be as comfortable as possible, you are much more assured of success if you draw up a floor plan with which you can experiment. It should be drawn to scale from the actual measurements of the room, but it is not nearly so scary to do as it sounds. You will, in any case, need a floor plan if, for example, you are devising a lighting and wiring plan from scratch (see page 30). Years ago, I came across explicit and easy-to-follow instructions in a book by designer Emily Malino called *Super Living Rooms* (Random House, 1976), and I have followed her recipe—and, indeed, advice—ever since. It went pretty much like this.

## HOW TO CREATE A FLOOR PLAN

To create a floor plan you will need:

- a 12-foot (3.6 m) folding yardstick or a 12-foot (3.6-m) recoiling tape (though the yardstick is easier for measuring ceilings, doors, and windows) or a more expensive—but very useful—scale ruler that automatically converts feet into inches, half inches, and quarter inches. Such a rule also makes it possible to measure inches more accurately than graph paper boxes, which can sometimes make a crucial difference to a room.
- several sheets of oversize quarter-inch graph paper, which has four squares to the inch or, if you have the scale ruler, several oversize sheets of plain paper
- a portable drawing board or a large piece of regular Masonite onto which you can attach the paper
- several sharp pencils and a good eraser (better than pens because you can then correct mistakes)
- some sheets of thin cardboard that are a different color from the paper, and a pair of sharp scissors to cut them accurately (to stand in for furniture, etc.)

## HOW TO MEASURE

First make a rough outline of the shape of the room, leaving gaps for the windows, doors, and any fireplace. Then measure everything in inches and write it down that way wherever relevant on the rough room shape. This obviates the chance of mixing up feet and inches if you are jotting them down in haste. You can always convert the inches to feet and inches when you are making the final plan.

Begin with the overall dimensions and try to find a spot where you can comfortably measure from wall to wall without running into any pieces of furniture or immovable objects. Measure both the length and width of the room from the floor and from baseboard to baseboard (since the feet or bases of furniture usually meet the molding rather than the wall).

## Comfort Zoning
### MEASURING BASICS

People often talk about a "rule of thumb," meaning a rough guide or principle. In fact, if you find yourself needing to measure something without the benefit of a tape measure, you can take the expression quite literally because you can pretty well reckon that the length between the last joint of your thumb to the edge of your fingernail is approximately one inch long. Similarly, the average adult foot is, curiously enough, about 1 foot long.

COMFORT TO ME IS A
ROOM THAT WORKS FOR
YOU AND YOUR GUESTS.
IT'S DEEP UPHOLSTERED
FURNITURE. ITS HAVING
A TABLE HANDY TO
PUT DOWN A DRINK
OR A BOOK. IT'S ALSO
KNOWING THAT IF
SOMEONE PULLS UP
A CHAIR FOR A TALK,
THE WHOLE ROOM DOES
NOT FALL APART.
I'M TIRED OF CONTRIVED
DECORATING.

AMERICAN DECORATOR
BILLY BALDWIN

When you have written down the room dimensions, start to measure the walls. Begin in one corner and measure to the nearest door, window, closet, bookcase, alcove, or column and note down the measurements of these as well. Continue along the wall in this way, measuring every feature, whether it is flat or at right angles to the wall. When you get to a window or door, measure the trim or molding separately as well as the actual glass or door, since you do not want, to have pieces of furniture overlapping trim or molding if you can help it. Do the same thing for all of the walls.

**HOW TO DRAW A FLOOR PLAN**

Once all the measurements have been noted, you can fix your paper to your drawing board or piece of Masonite, and start to work on the actual plan using either a half-inch- or a quarter-inch-per-foot scale. It is at this stage that you should start converting the inches into feet and inches.

When you complete the actual scale drawing of the full length of the first wall, check the total length against the overall room dimensions you noted before you started on the individual parts of the wall. If your room is perfectly rectangular, it should match exactly, give or take an eighth inch or so. Do the same thing when you have drawn the first width of the room. Don't be alarmed about quarter-inch discrepancies. Builders are sometimes careless and parallel walls might differ as much as an inch from each other. After you have cross-checked all dimensions and they match, you will know you are on the right track. If the dimensions of parallel walls turn out to be quite different, however, you have clearly made a mistake and you will need to retrace your movements.

To finish the drawing of any room you will need to indicate the architectural features with special recognized symbols. A window, for example, is drawn with two parallel lines close together. A door is drawn ajar, indicating where it hinges and which way it opens. A sliding door is indicated with two parallel lines like a window, but overlapped a little at the center.

## HOW TO PLAN A FURNITURE ARRANGEMENT

When you are satisfied that your plan is finalized and drawn to scale, you can start to finesse the actual furniture arrangement. You can buy kits with generic pieces of furniture already drawn to scale, which are certainly very helpful. But if you want to do your own, and get it really accurate to the last inch, the easiest way is to cut furniture shapes to the right scale out of thin cardboard and move them around within the floor plan until you have found the arrangement that seems to work the best. *Don't forget to label them.*

Proceed by measuring each piece you already own in exactly the way you measured the walls, in other words, the length and width in inches. But also make note of the various heights. Using your scale ruler, convert these into quarter-inch or half-inch scale outlines, cut them out, and label or code them.

Next make shapes for the furniture you hope to buy. If you have already made up your mind as to what you are going to acquire, it is easy enough to measure pieces at the store or antique shop, or to ask for the measurements. If you know what *kind* of pieces you want but have not yet picked out anything specific, try to measure or get measurements of similarly scaled pieces. Upholstered pieces are pretty standard, as are tables.

When you have got all your pieces of cardboard together and labeled, you can start fiddling around with the actual arrangement ideas; but bear in mind that there are three basic criteria that should be followed for true success. They are:

1 **Scale,** or the relationship of the size and shape of a piece of furniture to its space and to other pieces of furniture.

2 **Function,** or how people will use the furniture for conversation, or work, or relaxation.

3 **Traffic patterns,** or the space or paths between pieces of furniture in a room for people to pass through.

*Even if a room has a lively mix of color and pattern, if the furniture is all of the same height the overall effect can be tedious. Vary the look with a combination of tall lamps, plants, or an arrangement of large and small paintings and prints.*

# Elevations

To see how a grouping will look on or against a wall, you can draw it all on an elevation, or full frontal sketch of how your various walls might look. To do this, measure a wall exactly as you did the floor, except that for a wall you must also measure its height and width, as well as the heights of windows, doors, other openings or alcoves, radiators, and any furniture or accessories you want to use. Draw the wall on a sheet of paper with all of its various doors, windows, and so on, again to scale.

Now, suppose you want to place a low sofa along that wall with some other pieces that will add height to the space. Draw the length and the height of the sofa in the form of a rectangle on your elevation. Draw the height and width of any side tables or tall floor lamps and see how they look. Is the lamp too tall? Not tall enough? Erase it and try a different scale, or add a plant much the same size on the other side of the sofa. Or just add two tall table lamps to the side tables instead. Try to add in a good-sized painting over the sofa, or a block of prints that will approximate much the same size. What looks best? It is only by experimenting like this that you see what could work without having all the expense of money and effort beforehand.

Such elevations are also excellent for planning storage units or whole walls of storage to accommodate stereo, DVD player, CDs, tapes, TV, books, magazines, games, toys, files, collections of this and that, and all the other scattered detritus of family life that is much better well-ordered and hidden away than not. Once you know the measurements of the various storage units that are available and what items they are designed to hold, you can work out on paper exactly what would be best to buy and what all of your many diverse items they can store, thus avoiding many annoying, not to mention expensive, mistakes. Equally, if you want custom-built shelves and cupboards, you can, with your plan, give a carpenter or cabinetmaker a very good idea of exactly what you want.

Another very good use for elevations is to work out how best to hang your art and anything else hangable. Again measure your paintings, prints, framed photographs, mirrors, and so on and play around with their positions. This will save an awful lot of stops and starts and unwanted nail holes later. An equally good way to arrange art, however, is to try it out first on the floor immediately in front of the wall you are going to use.

LEFT: *An abrupt variation in height can be as visually arresting as a striking color or pattern. The sudden shift from low-level sofas to tall mirrored cabinet makes this room appear dynamic despite its neutral color scheme.*

OPPOSITE: *When planning walls for storage, TV, bookshelves, and so forth, it is a good idea to draw an elevation. To do this, measure the height and width of your walls and all of the various elements—windows, doors, etc.—and then purchase units to fit within those dimensions.*

**Scale** There is no doubt that the size of a piece of furniture can look disconcertingly different in different rooms. This is inclined to make scale a puzzling concept for those without the experience, and even with experience it is easy to make a mistake. That is why taking the trouble to make a floor plan with the furniture drawn to scale, and then experimenting, makes such a difference. Always take your floor plan with you when going shopping for items and always check the measurements of any new possibility against that plan before making a purchase.

It is a good idea too to measure your front door, inside doors (including size of the opening when the door itself is removed), stairs, windows (as last resort), and/or elevators before a purchase, and again to remember to cross-check the item's measurements. All too often, large mirrors, beds, large pieces of furniture, and paintings cannot be delivered successfully because they are too big, though sometimes, with a lot of effort, they can be brought in through a window opening of the room in question. It's hard to do, of course, in an apartment building, since hoists and goodness knows what else are involved.

Talking of which, there is also the fact that scale has a third dimension—height. And varying heights makes a surprising difference in any room. So much furniture is of much the same height, it can make a room look boring. But variation in height is as arresting as a stand-out color or pattern. So try to vary the pace with one or two tall pieces such as bookcases or an armoire or a secretary-desk; tall plants, tall skinny floor lamps, a piece of sculpture, or a bust on a plinth; one large painting or an arrangement of watercolors, prints, framed photographs; or a combination.

ABOVE: *An anchor seat or sofa with room behind its back functions as a space divider. Here, the seat is placed at a right angle to the focal point—the fireplace—with the balustrade functioning as a wall separating the seating area from the stairs.*

OPPOSITE: *Sofas, tables, and chairs should be arranged to create comfortable spots for reading, relaxing, or listening to music. Tables can be used to hold reading materials or game boards during the day, and cleared to act as a bar or serving space in the evening.*

**Function** Remember that the pieces of furniture you either possess or hope to possess will function in three ways: as anchors, as space dividers, as "communicators." And they must be placed in such a way that there will be at least one good, uncluttered "traffic" path for easy getting around.

The most important piece or pieces in a furniture arrangement are the so-called "anchors." Every room needs at least one such piece whose size and scale will give the space in general—and any grouping around it of lighter, more mobile pieces—a sense of stability. Pieces such as sofas, pianos, large tables, armoires, bureau and secretary bookcases, bookcases, storage units, and beds are anchors. Club or armchairs, occasional chairs, side tables, coffee or cocktail tables, benches, and so on are "floaters." Many years ago, I had a whole hour to myself on one of the old Phil Donahue TV shows. They built a living room and a bedroom in the studio, each of which I was supposed to decorate and furnish in front of the audience in three different ways. The living room had to be first traditional, then modern, then eclectic. The bedroom had to be first feminine, then masculine, then unisex. In the bedroom there was a window and a queen-sized bed. In the living room, a window, a fireplace, and a large sofa. These were the anchor pieces which always stayed. And around these same pieces I had to build my six different looks with all kinds of "floating" pieces, different lights, art, and accessories. Changing the wall decoration was like a strip-tease act with one treatment only loosely attached over the top of the other, to be ripped off when finished with. It was quite a detailed exercise that needed meticulous preparation and an extremely helpful group of stagehands/helpers with excellent memories.

In real life, the first thing you usually do is look for a focal point: a fireplace, or alternatively a large window with a view, or if all else fails, a (hopefully really well-designed) flat, wall-mounted plasma TV screen or one that perhaps can be concealed in some sort of armoire or cabinet (also well-designed) when not in use. Usually, this focus is on one of the long side walls and, depending on the width of the room, you normally look for a big enough piece of unbroken wall opposite this focal point to place a sofa and its attendant companion pieces, or floaters. If no such piece of wall exists (or if the room is really big), you will need to place, or can place, the sofa somewhere in the middle of the room, at right angles or opposite to the focal point, whether it is a fireplace, window, or whatever. A free-standing sofa, with room behind its back for another piece or pieces of furniture, creates its own division within a room. Depending upon the size of the space, you could have a sofa table behind the sofa with good lamps on it for anyone on the sofa to read by, and an arrangement of objects or piles of books. Or you could have a games or bridge table and some occasional chairs. Or you could make a quiet corner for listening to music, or reading, or just plain relaxing, with a reclining chair or club chair with a stool. And then again, you could put a desk and chair there. There are a number of possibilities. If the focal point is on an

end wall, you are then able to create two seating groups, one at each end, divided maybe by something in the middle, such as a large round library table, a low storage unit, a sofa, or even, if the room is large enough, two sofas back-to-back.

When you talk about a room "divider," furniture that divides the space, you often envision a shelving system, bookcases, or some other device such as columns or overscale plants that make a demarcation line between one part of a room and another. But a free-standing sofa, or sofas, in the middle of the room is not only an important anchor piece but a divider as well. There are various other pieces that can be used for this same function. If, for example, you also eat in the living room, you could use a round table, which could be used for books and so on by day, or a low storage piece that can act as a bar or serving space on one side and a "wall" on the other and that will effectively divide off living and eating space without interrupting the apparent flow of space. If the piece is not well-finished at the back, you could tile it or cover it with plywood that can then be stained or faux painted. The top can be used to hold plants, a lamp or pair of lamps, sculpture, or some sort of grouping of objects that will look decorative from both sides and still leave room for serving drinks or food.

Furniture can also communicate its own function. Pieces of furniture act as communicators via their placing and their relationship to one other. If you are creating a classic U-shaped conversation group, for example, you might place

*To create a conversation group, place chairs on either side or at an angle to your anchor sofa, then place a table in between to rest glasses, reading material, and so on. If you have the space, add a comfy window seat to extend the sitting area.*

two low club chairs or armchairs to one side of your anchor sofa, at a right angle to it, with a small table in between them to support a possible lamp and to provide a useful space for placing glasses, cups and saucers, and so on. You might then put a couple of occasional chairs, again with a table between them, opposite the armchairs and on the other side of the table. You would add a low coffee table in front of the sofa and maybe a lamp table on either side. You will then have created an obvious and comfortable place for general conversation, with ample room for seven or eight people. If the room is large, you could replace the two occasional chairs with a love seat (with tables on either side), and have the occasional chairs, again with a table between them, opposite the sofa to form a kind of square but with room for people to walk around and get in and out of the conversational loop without causing a disturbance. And remember that corners are excellent places to display sculpture and plants lit by up-lights, as well as secondary pieces of furniture—from corner cupboards to a couple of chairs and a round table to make a secondary conversation group; or a chair, footstool, small low table, and lamp (especially for reading); or an étagère for the display of objects.

**Traffic Patterns** It is, of course, necessary to leave a kind of path in any room for people to walk through and get to relevant seating. The path does not need to cut a huge swathe through the furniture arrangement—in fact, it is quite rare for two people to walk through a living room side by side, or even following each other, except in party situations, and then all furniture is usually moved aside anyway. A 3-foot (.9-m) clear run is a reasonable space to leave. Thoughts of traffic should also be applied to the distance between pieces of furniture and the space between furniture and walls. A coffee table, for example, should not be farther than 1 foot 6 inches (.5 m) from the sofa or chairs it serves. This will allow enough space for people to move through the two pieces but not so much that it is awkward to lean forward to reach for a glass or book. Another good rule is to allow 2 feet 6 inches to 3 feet (.8 to .9 m) behind the backs of chairs around a dining table to allow people to pass around dishes and to get in and out of their chairs comfortably. Bear these space measurements in mind when filling in your furniture arrangement plans. If the plan starts to look crowded, remeasure the clearances more carefully.

## FURNITURE

There is little doubt that when most people first think of comfort in a living room or family room, they think of comfortable seating. They think of upholstery that they can sink into, deep armchairs and sofas, or chaises that will both support and cosset their probably weary limbs and backs; a useful and generous side table within easy reach of their hand for dumping a drink or a book; good reading light; and footstools of a convenient height on which they can rest their feet.

BOOKCASES FULL OF BOOKS, SHELVES FULL OF MUSICAL EQUIPMENT AND DISKS, STORAGE WALLS WITH A PLACE FOR EVERYTHING AND EVERYTHING IN ITS PLACE ARE ALL COMMUNICATORS IN THEIR OWN RIGHT, SINCE THEY PROCLAIM THE INTERESTS OF THEIR OWNERS. SO ARE THE ART AND OBJECTS IN A ROOM, AND EVEN THE PLANTS AND FLOWERS.

*Corner cupboards and tables are wonderful for displaying plants, flowers, sculpture, and other works of art. Any display should be properly thought out, with items looking neat and uncluttered.*

But what they forget is that it is rare for one generic chair or sofa to suit every type of body. So much depends on height, length of legs, and the state of one's back, not to mention one's mind. Some people prefer firmness. Others prefer softness. Some people prefer sofas and chairs with a tight seat and back and no loose pillows. Others prefer to sink into and onto the squishiness of feather-stuffed cushions, with the seat cushions perhaps filled with a foam core as well as the feathers for more firmness. Others have an allergy to feathers and need a synthetic fiber. Some people (with long legs) like a deep seat and cushioned back. Others (with shorter legs) need a shallower seat, or a whole lot more loose pillows to stuff behind them. People with bad backs and older people find higher seats more comfortable, with firm arms to aid them in sitting down and getting up.

Happily, there seems to be something for all requirements. If you cannot find exactly what you want in stores (and like buying a mattress, you must really spend enough time trying out for comfort everything you like the shape of), good manufacturers are invariably willing, via a salesperson, to adapt their designs to customer preferences—if, that is, you do not mind waiting a couple of months or more. (By the way, you most likely would have to do this anyway, since very few firms except places such as Ikea keep large upholstered pieces in stock.) If you entertain a lot,

*For centuries, love seats, ottomans, and large square floor cushions have served as comfortable and stylish seating. This scarlet settee with carved legs makes a stunning center-piece to this leisure-time room.*

*Old and new pieces can be successfully married to have the best of both worlds. The decorative pillow on this antique day bed makes the seat more welcoming while unifying the color and patterns of the painting and rug.*

or if your family contains older people or taller or shorter ones, it would be wise to consider getting several different types of chairs to accommodate their various needs.

There are also, of course, many firms of upholsterers (often old family firms) that will make exactly what you want in whatever size you request, as well as adapting, modifying, and reupholstering older pieces. Although it is generally thought that it is less expensive to start anew, this is mostly not so, because it is often difficult to locate good new frames, while a good upholsterer can square off old pieces that are too rounded, round out pieces that are too squared, add or subtract rolled arms and backs, and add fringes, tufting or button-backs, ruching, trims, and every sort of slipcover. This is great for people who have inherited furniture, who have family heirlooms that are not particularly comfortable by today's standards, or who have picked up old chairs and sofas from yard sales. All these gifts and finds can be given a new and more comfortable lease on life.

## SOFAS, LOVE SEATS, AND ARMCHAIRS

Genre paintings, drawings, and engravings all through the centuries show banquettes, divans, ottomans, stools, and large square floor cushions for seating, all covered in fabric (and most often stuffed with horsehair). Although there were actually a few rare seventeenth-century sofas, including the famous and still popular Knole version with its high back and equally high let-down sides (still to be seen at Knole, the sixteenth-century house in Kent, England, belonging to the Sackville-West family)—and, of course, a good many eighteenth- and early nineteenth-century couches and settees with somewhat spindly or curved legs—large, comfortable upholstered pieces did not really come into use before the second half of the nineteenth century, after the advent of springs in the 1830s. Men's clubs were some of the first establishments to invest in these pieces, and in the United States, comfortable armchairs are called "club chairs" to this day.

Interestingly, most of the designs used in the nineteenth century—and some of the pre-spring shapes of the eighteenth century—have endured into this century with only subtle modifications. The *Knole* sofa already mentioned is sold both in its original form and in a long, low-backed version known as the *St. Thomas* sofa, with squared-off arms the same height and sewn-on pillow-like pads overlapping the long seat cushion. The *Camelback* sofa, with its irregularly shaped back (a bump that looks like a camel's hump), was a design much used by furniture designers such as Chippendale and Hepplewhite and is still popular today. So is the late eighteenth-century *Martha Washington* chair (also known invitingly as a *lolling* chair), with its low upholstered seat, open arms, and high upholstered back. The *Chesterfield* sofa, a tufted sofa with back and arms the same size, has not changed in style or name since Victorian days. The *Bridgewater* chair, with its softly curved arm, has been going for generations. And so has the *Morris* chair, named after the British Arts & Crafts designer William Morris, which has arms extending slightly behind the back that can be adjusted to various angles. There has also been a substantial revival of other nineteenth-century armchairs with short legs and curved backs that are surprisingly comfortable.

Do not forget either the comfortable day beds with arms, the modern version of the old *chaises longues,* or long chairs, first introduced in the seventeenth century.

On the whole, you can quite safely marry new and generously sized upholstery pieces with a collection of antique and traditional furniture for the best of both

ABOVE: *Roomy and relaxing armchairs play a necessary role in a room that aspires to be comfortable. Change the upholstery or slipcover fabric to fit your design needs.*

RIGHT: *Even formal sofas can be generously cushioned for distinctive comfort. This elegant, long couch is beautifully accessorized with coordinating pillows in large and small sizes.*

*Placed against a long side wall, a flat, wall-mounted plasma TV screen can serve as the focal point of the room. Surround the TV with sofas and chairs at a good distance for unobstructed viewing.*

worlds. Many people still seem to feel that it is best to use those tight-covered, elegantly legged and framed late eighteenth- and early nineteenth-century couches to accompany fine cabinetry; but however elegant they are, there is nothing inviting or welcoming about them, even if they are covered with small pillows. Such pieces often really come into their handsome own in a bedroom, perhaps at the foot of a bed, where they can be more for show than comfort. Anyway, they make good resting places at night for all the small decorative pillows with which so many beds are decked. Another thing to bear in mind is that some of the hard-edged modern sofas and chairs *look* less than comfortable, even if they are. And, as I have said, it is preferable to have pieces that are as comforting to the eye as they are comfortable to lounge on. There is no need to sacrifice comfort for style. If a modern room lacks any sort of natural focal point, you might think of installing some of the deeply comfortable modular units and upholstered stools, because they can be used to create an effective room within a room.

## OCCASIONAL CHAIRS

Occasional chairs, or chairs light enough and good-looking enough to be moved around to supplement conversational seating groups when needed and to fit in with other antique, traditional, or modern furniture, play a most necessary role in a room that purports to be comfortable.

When the first *Regence* and *Louis XV Bergeres* (lightly padded armchairs with open spaces between the arms and the seat) were introduced in France, they were pronounced the most comfortable of seats. Indeed, the many reproductions and versions of the same design have remained comfortable, and correspondingly popular, to this day.

Other occasional chairs are nineteenth-century *library* chairs and their reproductions, which have high-ish backs; straight-sided arms; short, slightly curved saber legs at the back; and short, straight legs at the front. A small pillow or two

## Comfort Zoning
### FURNITURE BASICS

Do not worry about mixing antique furniture and squashy, deeply comfortable modern upholstery. If the comfortable pieces available now had been available in the eighteenth and early nineteenth centuries, our ancestors would have ordered them like a shot—just as they would have availed themselves of modern lighting, heating, insulation, and plumbing.

makes them both more comfortable to look at and to sit in. They often have casters or wheels and, because they are comparatively light, they are again quite easy to maneuver.

*Slipper* chairs—small, armless, low, curved-back chairs with regular-sized seats on short legs—were originally designed in eighteenth-century France to set by the fire in the bedroom or boudoir to keep ladies warm while they were putting on their expensive and fragile silk stockings. At that time they were called *chauffeuses* and had curved backs and delicate frames (though the word, of course, had to do with keeping warm rather than with lady drivers). However, a century later, the Victorians took the basic idea of dwarf chairs, so to speak, but made them both sturdier and more fanciful so that they could be dropped pretty well anywhere in a room as an extra piece of amusing but nonconfrontational seating that would take up the minimum of space. Sometimes they had turned legs, sometimes cabriole legs, sometimes upholstered legs and a fixed loose cushion; sometimes they had tufted backs and pleated skirts with no legs showing at all.

In the 1950s and 1960s, the well-known decorator Billy Baldwin, mentor and inspiration to so many of today's designers, got rid of the curves and straightened the backs, topping them with simple slipcovers, often with equally simple contrasting braid or tape trims. Now many of the Victorian curved and tufted versions have been reincarnated. Usually they have some sort of skirt either shirred or with inverted corner pleats, or box pleats, although they can be tight-covered

*A comfy chaise lounge, a well-placed reading light, and a roomy side table transform an unassuming corner into a relaxing retreat.*

LEFT: *Ergonomically designed chairs are attractive in a modern living room. With its tall windows, clean lines, and vivid colors, this contemporary room looks especially fresh and inviting.*

BELOW: *Enhance your leisure room with vases and pots of fresh flowers and plants. Look for flowers with bright colors and delicious scents to add a finishing touch to your living room, as well as every room of your home.*

and given quite modern legs. In any event, in whatever guise, and in whatever style of room, they are extremely useful as extra comfortable chairs to expand a seating group or to set by a fire without blocking it.

## FINISHING TOUCHES

Whatever furniture, furnishings, objects, and art you may possess, and however well they are arranged, they can only be enhanced by vases and jugs of fresh flowers, and well-tended plants. Lilies, narcissi, fresh lavender, old-fashioned roses, sweet peas, gardenias, and jasmine in season are wonderfully comforting to the olfactory senses, as are tendrils of jasmine surrounding windows, beds of nicotiana or tobacco plants or night-scented stocks under open living room windows on summer evenings. A good second are window boxes planted with delicious smelling or deliciously colored flowers.

Keeping rooms consistently freshly aired and clean is important too. I have already mentioned the charm of sweet-smelling wood on the fire. But here too scented candles are nice, particularly at night, as well as bowls of sweet-smelling potpourri put here and there on tables and ledges, and an occasional dash or two of lavender essence on rugs and carpets.

And there is one final thing. A sense of detail plays a great part in a memorable home. This extends not just to keeping a room—actually, the whole home—fresh and clean, tidy, warm or cool according to climate, full of fresh flowers and healthy plants, not to mention with everything in good order, but it also means trying to ensure that minor details such as hardware for doors, light switches, and so on are well chosen. They are small things certainly, but details add up in the final picture.

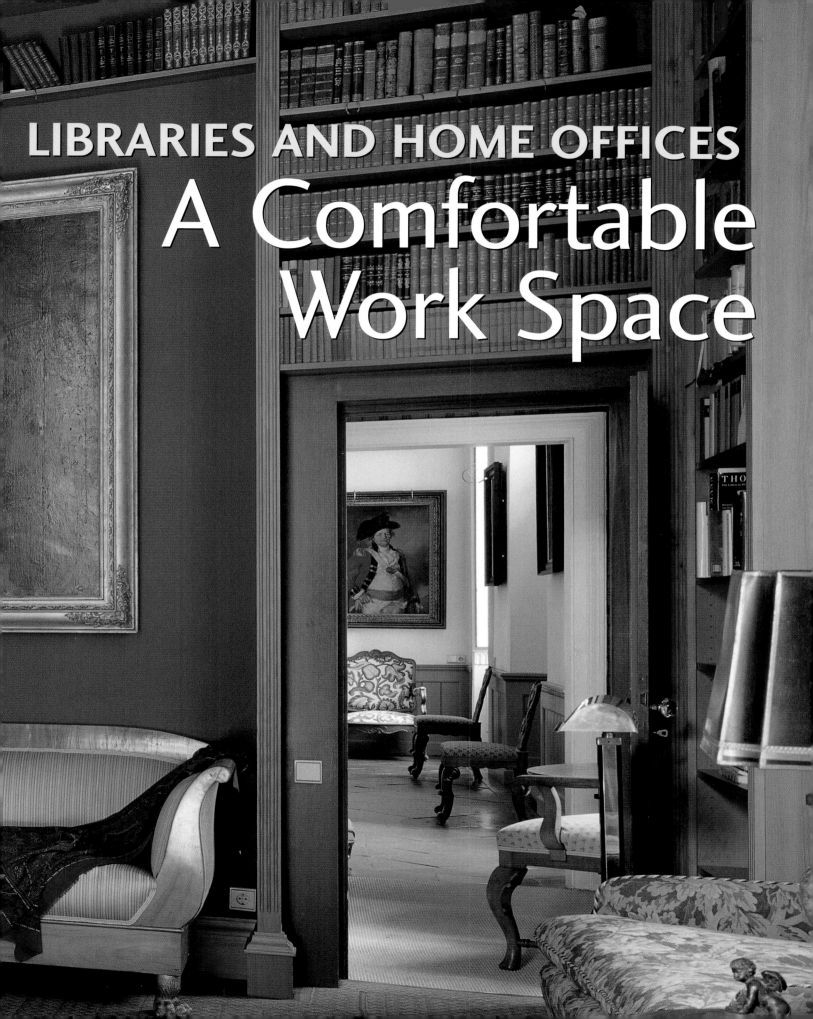

# A Comfortable Work Space

*Domestic libraries—and I would include the smaller studies within this term—have long been a favorite room for those lucky enough to possess such a space.*

More intimate than living rooms, libraries are also easier to decorate, mostly because books and bookcases provide a good deal of decoration in themselves and generally require darker, warmer, comforting colors to set them off. Lately, home offices have become just as popular, and, in fact, a necessity in a household where owners have chosen to work from home.

In the last decade or two, with the rapid growth of personal computers, e-mail, the Internet, fax machines, and so on, not to mention better, more domesticated office furniture design, it has become much easier—and less expensive—for many people to work from home rather than undergo the tedious, frustrating, time-wasting, and often increasingly expensive trek to an office. Moreover, many employers welcome the chance of not having to provide more office space and equipment, not to mention the financial responsibilities of full-time employees.

Although people might, at first, miss the camaraderie of office life, the benefits of working at home—and the freedom to create one's own hours—soon outweigh the lack of office interaction. It is particularly pleasant to be able to sit down to work in an untrammeled way, in a comfortable chair at a clean and well-organized desk or writing table in a convenient room with everything at hand. In the so-called "good old days" (which were the good days for the then prosperous and more leisured classes), studies, libraries, and home offices for the few people who did work mostly from home—mainly farmers, writers, some editors, old-fashioned family doctors, and designers—were some of the easiest rooms to furnish, equip, and make comfortable to be in. They were mainly small, cozy rooms predicated toward the comfort and efficiency of one person, or at the most a couple, with the occasional guest.

The same tenets hold true for today's home offices. While few family homes nowadays can afford the luxury of a room given over solely as an office, wherever you work, your home office area should be generally comfortable, and possibly quirky. It should also follow much the same decorating guidelines as living rooms, with thoughtful lighting (you will want to light bookshelves and work, and have chairside lamps for reading and ambient lighting), comfortable seating, an entertainment center for a TV, DVD/VCR player, et. al., a good desk, good storage, and almost always a lot of books. Walls are often dark, with rich or warm colors, sometimes covered in fabric (see page 40). Even in the dedicated home office (as opposed to a time share with another room) there should be space for books, even if they are mostly of the reference variety.

ABOVE: *A collection of architectural elements, antique finials, and lamp bases will add character to a formal library. Display groups of unusual or unique objects on shelves, tables, and desktops.*

OPPOSITE: *Libraries generally require darker, warmer colors, as books generally look better against darker walls and furniture. Bookshelves made of fine woods, plush carpets, and long drapes make this library more private and peaceful.*

# Creating a Peaceful Library

*Theoretically, the purpose of a home library is to house and read books. So, quite naturally, the bookshelves themselves go a long way in furnishing the room. Shelves can run from floor to ceiling, with the rest of the wall space given over to art.*

IN THE COMFORT AND
COMFORTING STAKES,
I WOULD PUT GOOD
COLLECTIONS OF BOOKS
RIGHT UP THERE ALONG
WITH THE FIREPLACE,
AND PREFERABLY BOTH
TOGETHER.

Libraries, although dedicated theoretically toward the housing of individually collected and treasured books and the peaceful reading of them, often end up as dual-purpose space for dining as well—which certainly makes a pleasant background for the diners—or as a kind of adult family room away from the family, or as a more private and quieter sitting room.

## BOOKSHELVES

It is interesting how often one sees rooms designated as libraries in decorating magazines with hardly a book to be seen. Not even perfectly bound books-by-the-yard. Yet bookshelves and their contents go a very long way toward furnishing a room. So particular attention should be paid to the design and placing of them, as well as to their contents.

Whether the bookshelves are designed for a large or small library, a study, or a home office, care should be taken to integrate them into the general character of the room, particularly if it possesses some pleasant architectural details such as good-looking cornices and baseboards. If there are no particular details and the ceiling is flat, you could take the shelves to right under the ceiling so that the top framing of the shelves form a cornice in themselves. But if you want to show off an existing cornice, or you have old uneven ceilings, you will need to leave a gap between ceiling and top shelf that is preferably big enough for the display of urns, busts, sculpture, pieces of porcelain, a lined-up collection of framed prints, watercolors, photographs, or anything else that you think might suit the space.

Some bookshelves are built to go behind the furniture and are given their own baseboards, or baseboards that match those on other walls if the room is not book-lined. If the room is completely book-lined, it is the wood or color of the bookshelves and the spines of the books, especially if they are mellow old ones, that provide both the coloring and, in their way, the decoration of the room. The kaleidoscope of colors given by modern books has its own somewhat careless charm, though I once saw an especially soothing book-lined room in New York City where each book had been covered in heavy cream parchment and all the titles and authors' names (not necessarily, I am afraid, the publishers) had been painstakingly written out in beautiful calligraphic writing in brown ink. British decorator David Hicks filled bookshelves in one of his rooms with nothing but books with red bindings because "they looked better like that." And the owner of a house in France I went to write about was quite beside herself when she came back from a trip and found that all her books carefully organized by subject and author had been reorganized by a house-sitting friend in careful blocks of color.

In a large library, if anyone is fortunate enough to possess one, back-to-back shelves can be built to come out at right angles every so often to provide charming sitting alcoves. I say "back-to-back" because the plain back of a single bookshelf, unless painted, fabriced, or wallpapered to blend in with any non-bookcase-covered wall, would look unsightly, whereas bookcases back-to-back between two such seating alcoves would be both handsome and useful.

In, say, a library-dining room, some bays of shelves could come down to the baseboards; others, designated as breakfronts, could come to the height of the windowsill or sills, with cabinets fronted either by paneled doors or close grille-work underneath, some to hold papers and files, some to hold dining room china and glass. One or two walls could be left unshelved to accommodate a handsome early nineteenth-century mahogany breakfront bookcase perhaps, or a secretary-

*If the room is completely book-lined, the color of the book spines can provide the coloring as well as the decoration of the room. The books can be arranged in a relaxed, casual manner, or carefully organized by subject matter or even by height or color.*

bookcase that can also be used as the desk for the room—again using a cabinet or shelves underneath for china and glass storage as well as papers, or partially for table linens and for papers if there are drawers. The shelves in the upper cabinet could either be used for more books as originally intended, or to hold the best glass or pieces of porcelain or some sort of collection. The rest of the wall space could be given over to art.

Not all bookshelves however, have to be specially built for the space. I have seen quite run-of-the-mill, off-the-rack shelves successfully "built-in" with the aid of painted infills of Sheetrock. In any event, whether shelves are bought or custom-built, try to match the size of the bays of shelves to some other architectural element in the room such as the door or windows. But always make sure that shelves are made from thick pieces of wood and are not too long, so that they do not sag or dip under the weight of books, or if they are a bit longer than practicable because of a window size, that they are well-supported in the middle.

*In addition to books, library shelves can be used to display small sculptures, decorative vases, framed works of art, and such. These decorative items can act as bookends, supporting and separating rows of books on the individual shelves.*

*This handsome breakfront bookcase is painted to blend with the wall color as well as the other furnishings in the room. The cabinet underneath is useful for storing papers, binders, and albums.*

If bookshelves are made from some beautiful wood or other, all well and good; but if they are not, as is most often the norm, then they can be painted, either to blend in with the rest of the walls or to stand out as a contrast. Any paneling could then be picked out with different tones, or not, as the case maybe. And do not forget those useful small, waist-high bookshelves either, which also look good against walls with collections of this and that, or plants, on the top ledges.

## LIGHTING

I have talked about the need for good reading, work, and ambient lighting on pages 30–33, so here I will focus on lighting up bookshelves. This is a good thing; but although some people build an overhang at the top of bookshelves or a storage wall, these mostly only light the top shelves rather than graze all the spines of the books or the contents of shelves so that you can see quickly what you want. The most efficient way, if you can do it, is to recess angled wall washers into the ceiling about 30 inches (76 cm) back from the wall, or put in some sort of track or inconspicuous stretched wire and attendant spots.

## WINDOWS

Depending upon the size of the relevant windows, libraries have much the same window treatment choices as living rooms. If you have any rare books, they will need corresponding special care, so here you will always need efficient shades that can ward off or filter strong sunlight, either instead of or in addition to curtains or draperies.

IT IS TRADITIONAL TO HAVE AT LEAST ONE PIECE OF LEATHER-UPHOLSTERED SEATING IN LIBRARIES AND STUDIES, EITHER AS A CLUB CHAIR OR A SOFA; BUT WHETHER OR NOT YOU CHOOSE LEATHER, IT IS A GOOD IDEA TO CHOOSE COLORS AND ACCESSORIES THAT MELD IN, RATHER THAN COMPETE, WITH THE BOOKS.

RIGHT: *While libraries are, for the most part, most comforting filled with familiar and traditional items, a shot of the unexpected, like this swirling sculptured plant, can lend a note of whimsy to an otherwise formal space.*

BELOW: *In addition to ambient light, a library should most definitely have good reading lights. Lamps should be set so that the light shines down on the desk surface to illuminate reading materials without glare.*

## COLORS

If rich or warm colors are the convention for libraries and their smaller relations, studies, it is for a good reason. Books generally do look better against darker walls and furniture, and darker walls are undoubtedly cocooning. In cooler climates you can run through the gamut of reds, terra-cottas, deep camel sparked with reds, greens from emerald to dark leaf, marmalade through tobacco to a rich deep brown, and deep navy to a rich ultramarine.

All of these colors look good on shelves as well as walls (if the wood is inexpensive), or contrasted with the grain of fine woods, or spiced with white. Rich, intense (but not necessarily always darker) colors are appropriate in warmer climates too, although here the reds usually give way to the range of greens from apple and grass to laurel, and to periwinkle and dark blues, and the browns from oatmeal to caramel to dark chestnut.

## WALLS

When much of the walls are covered by bookshelves, it would be affordable to make a library even more cocooning by covering any wall space that is left with fabric: wall felts or burlaps, which are available in a large choice of appealing colors as well as being paper-backed so they can be used like wallpapers. Various suede-effects are popular again in a range of natural shades with some dyed colors, as are leathers. Alternatively, more exotic fabrics such as linen velvet or corduroy or slubbed silk or heavy cottons can be stretched over thin wood lathes lined with a special padding, called "bump" in the trade, that makes walls almost as soft to look at as to touch.

## FLOORING

Since libraries and studies are presumed to be quiet spaces, they are best close carpeted or covered in wool sisal, regular sisal, coir or some sort of matting, or largely rugged over a handsome wood or tiled floor (depending on location and climate), either by one large carpet or by a succession of smaller rugs, which can easily be overlapping to give a rather exotic look.

## ACCESSORIES

Libraries and studies are good spaces for collections. If most or nearly all of the wall area is taken up by bookshelves, collections of this and that can be displayed on the shelves along with, or among, or in front of the books, as can small paintings and prints or photographs. If there is wall space, it often looks good to group a whole series of prints, or drawings, or small paintings or photographs or a mixture, as opposed to rather thinly spreading single paintings around—unless, of course, they are especially large or precious. Historically, such rooms are sympathetic to sculpture, busts, plaster casts, and large globes, although they still look just as handsome if conventional. But there again, it is the familiar that most often imparts a sense of comforting solidity.

*All of the elements in a library—the furniture, accessories, lighting, and flooring—should work together to make the room a lovely retreat for moments of study, repose, and reflection.*

# Dual-Purpose Home Offices

## Comfort Zoning

### WALL OUTLET BASICS

Make sure you have extra electric outlets and a second (or third) phone line and outlets near wherever you plan to install a work space.

SOMETIMES IT IS MORE
A QUESTION OF HAVING
A DESK OF ONE'S OWN
THAN A ROOM.

If there is no possibility of installing a home office in a separate room, then plans have to be made that will cause the least upset in some other room. A guest room is preferable to one's own bedroom because, on the whole, one really wants a bedroom to be quite divorced from work. One good way of making a home office/guest room is to conceal all the work part in a group of closets along one wall with sliding or folding doors. Make sure there are electrical and phone outlets available for your computer, printer, and fax machine, as well as for a good desk light. Also, unless the room is likely to be used by a guest for days or weeks at a time, you can make the room look much more like a study by using a sofa bed rather than the regular variety.

Dining rooms, if they exist, are another good place. They are almost always used as dual-purpose rooms now anyway. The dining table can be used as a work surface, or a large desk can double as a serving table; and any cabinets can be shared for file and paper storage as well as for dining needs. If you are inclined to cause an overflow of papers, you can always put them in baskets and shove them under the table (as far as possible toward the center so as not to get in the way of diners' legs) when you need the room for eating in, and conceal it all with a floor-length tablecloth.

If you are forced to use a corner of the living room and need a lot of files and papers, it might again, as in a guest bedroom, be worth building a wall of cabinets that can also house a desk surface, computer, and other equipment. Alternatively, there are well-designed desks and worktables with integral storage for files and so on designed especially for corners, and they would be worth searching out. Again, do not forget to have enough phone and electrical outlets installed near the workplace.

The space under the stairs—if there is one—is always a neat little area to install a desk, compact filing cabinets, and equipment. If you have a big enough landing area in the house, this too can be fitted out as a work space.

RIGHT: *If a separate room is not available, home offices can be installed in a bedroom, guest room, or living room. If this is the case, the desk area should be furnished and decorated in a style consistent with the rest of the room.*

OPPOSITE: *If you have set aside a corner of the living room for an office area, consider installing a wall of bookshelves and cabinets to store papers, files, supplies, and reference materials.*

# Creating an Organized Work Area

## HOME OFFICE DÉCOR

One thing to think about when planning a home work space, is that it really does not *have* to be an officey sort of office so to speak, at least looks-wise. Most professional offices have a hierarchy, a pecking order for employees to aspire to and a vested interest in appearing as professional as possible. A home work space should at least *work* professionally. It should also be separated as much as possible from the general workings of the house, especially if clients come to visit (it is not, after all, overly impressive for one's professional image to have to walk clients by the washing or leftover breakfast clutter or other signs of overt domesticity). However, the general design, as long as it works efficiently, can be as idiosyncratic as you like.

One psychologist client of mine, who decided to give up her (normal office-like) professional office space across town and transform the newly acquired studio apartment next door into an office, was forced to see patients in her home study until the new office was ready. The study, as it happened, had been originally designed as a kind of playful desert tent with painted striped tent sides and a "torn" opening in the

*While home offices do not need to look officey, it is a good idea to at least organize the space for both comfort and efficiency. This is especially true if the office is part of a communal living space, where piles of paperwork could intrude on daily living.*

"canvas" roof open to the sky. She made a visual division between this study and the living room, dining area, and kitchen with an open screen and a huge plant, and a "waiting" area down the hall with a cushioned bench, a small table for magazines, and a couple of small occasional chairs in a tiled alcove behind an unusual, or at least unexpected, working fountain that flowed gently and soothingly all day long. She was somewhat doubtful as to the way her patients would react, but was so delighted by their enthusiastic response to the fantasy that she decided to make the new office similarly fanciful but with a great deal of concealed storage space for files, really comfortable seating, and a generous footage of bookshelves for all her reference books. In other words, to combine a really useful functionalism with the exotic.

Not everyone would be so comfortable with this sort of departure from classic office style, but that is no reason to think that one should necessarily go the other way and import steel filing cabinets, standard gray contract carpeting, and a utilitarian desk and chair into the domestic setting.

## ORGANIZATION

In any room or space in the house where people work at home, files, periodicals, and papers are inclined to multiply more quickly than pigeons descending for scraps on a winter's day. So there is clearly a need for thoughtful storage to be squeezed in wherever possible. It is, therefore, the *organizational* part of the design that should be attended to first for comfort's sake, whether you are going to be doing professional or simply domestic paperwork. Particularly if the work space is definitely a more communal part of the home in the evenings and on weekends. Or, as is so often the case, if a home office has to be in a corner somewhere— on a landing; tucked under the stairs perhaps; or sharing a dining room, part of a kitchen, a guest bedroom, or, most inconvenient of all, a living room.

### MAXIMIZING STORAGE SPACE

Thoughtful organization means seriously maximizing storage space and using up every nook and cranny for closets or shelves. You will always need much more space to stash things away in than you could ever possibly imagine if you aspire to keep the room neat and clean.

Even if you do succumb to the utilitarian steel filing cabinets, remember that they can be painted an un-officelike color (ask someone at a good paint supply or hardware store to suggest the best paint for the purpose); or put castors or ball bearings below custom-built breakfront bookshelves so they can be slipped into cupboards and then easily pulled out for access. Alternatively, an attractive armoire or wardrobe can be converted inside to hold a mass of stuff. There are, of course, a number of individual and sensible stacking baskets and trays of different form and

*Even if the home office is designed solely for domestic paperwork, having a clear and well-organized work area is important. A drop-front secretary like this one offers practical storage yet closes for a neat appearance.*

TOP: *Instead of a traditional desk, a sturdy table can provide an attractive and capacious work area. If there are no drawers, work papers and files can be stored in portable stacking baskets or file carts.*

ABOVE: *Traditional office décor and desk accessory items include globes, maps, and so forth. Bookends and paperweights are attractive and useful, while wall hangings and framed art provide variety and personality.*

dimensions that look friendlier than filing cabinets, are inexpensive and practical, and can be used to store stationery, letters, files, and papers. Bigger baskets can hold slim files, and large box files can go in neat rows into bookcases. Since there are quite decorative-looking box files for sale now, they are well worth searching out. Office supplies and good stationery stores are now full of unexpected surprises.

## LIGHTING

I talked about work lights and their best positioning on pages 32–33, and of course it is important to have as good an adjustable desk light as you can afford, which will take the maximum possible voltage, preferably with a three-way or dimmer switch to lower the light when you are not using the space to work. If the room is a definite designated office, then you will want good ambient/background light as well. This can be provided by a table lamp or two on tables by the comfortable chair or chairs and small sofa that you will need for relaxing in, reading, or taking a quick nap when concentration at the desk starts to flag.

## WINDOWS

Home offices will look more businesslike with shutters or shades of some kind, whether picked from the vast choice of ready-made louvers, mini-blinds, matchsticks, wood Venetians, or whatever, or else custom-made roller or Roman shades.

## COLORS

If the home office is in its own space —as opposed to playing a dual role in another room—it can be colored in any way that suits you, or that seems crisp and fresh and cutting-edge. All white, or gray and white, or black and white, or the paler camels, greiges, and ecrus are conventionally businesslike. But there is no reason why you cannot use a primary color such as red or yellow or blue, or a bright apricot or green crisped up with white to express your independence of thought as well as location.

## FLOORING

Home offices, especially if they are meant to look efficient and businesslike as well as comfortable, can either be carpeted wall-to-wall with a neutral color (with or without a border that can add to the crisp look) or covered with wool or natural sisal. In a warm climate, rugs or mats on tile are quite acceptable as long as it is not too noisy.

## FURNITURE AND ACCESSORIES

When furnishing a home office or home work space, there are certain pieces of furniture that are essentials. Obviously a good, large, sturdy desk or work table will be necessary, especially if it is to provide a stable base for a computer, and there is now a very large choice of just such good-looking, purpose-built desks

in a variety of styles to hold computers, printers, fax machines, and telephones, as well as a maximum number of drawers. Also, the most comfortable and ergonomically designed desk chair is only sensible when you are spending long hours at a computer or simply writing longhand. And if there is room, it would be useful to have an armchair or love seat or both for reading and relaxing, as well as for receiving any clients who come to the home. Incidentally, if this is the case, make sure that powder rooms or washrooms are always kept clean and tidy so that they are equally welcoming for office visitors.

But if the cost of furnishing a work space with appropriate furniture and equipment seems daunting, don't despair. You can provide yourself with a sturdy and capacious work surface and many drawers and cupboards for storage by purchasing two or three (depending on space) unfinished wood chests of drawers, or a mixture of chests and drawers and cupboards, all the same height, and arranging them together against a long wall, leaving an appropriate kneehole or two. Top them with a length of laminated (easy-to-clean) block board or butcher block, and paint or lacquer them whatever color you please or just stain and varnish them.

It is really quite easy to find second-hand office chairs, not to mention computers, fax machines, printers, desk lamps, filing cabinets, and so on (which can also be painted to match a new work surface).

As far as accessories are concerned, home offices of the deliberately efficient variety are fine with charts, maps, photographs, bulletin boards, and the usual work accoutrements. The more idiosyncratic versions are again a good area for collections of this and that.

*A sturdy work table is an absolute necessity to provide a stable base for a computer, printer, fax machine, and so forth. Comfortable, ergonomically designed desk chairs are also a must if you plan on spending long hours at your work station.*

# Reds

RED IS A COLOR that works very well in dark rooms and in cool climates. In fact, it's been proven that people sitting in a red painted room feel warmer than those in a blue room kept at the same temperature. Even those who announce that they really could not feel comfortable living with the color should remember that no one color is just that. And although many people equate red primarily with the scarlet of fire engines, geraniums, or a heavy Victorian crimson, red is actually particularly rich in variations.

Just think . . . the red-purple of eggplants; the ruby and garnet of jewels; wine from Bordeaux to Burgundy; fall hips, spring pimpernels, and winter holly berries; red peppers, tomatoes, cherries, strawberries, raspberries, mulberries, cranberries, and rhubarb. And so many flowers: from the gamut of velvety rose hybrids to peonies, poppies, and pansies; to azaleas, bougainvillea, cyclamens, fuschias, geraniums, and then some, ranging from scarlet to the palest pinks. Think too of browny-reds such as Chinese sang de boeuf, or bull's blood, or that lovely deep Venetian red, or terracotta flowerpots, which range from pale reddish buff to a deep red-brown. Then there are earthy oranges and yellow-reds like bricks, which also range on the rosy side; the glowingly deep red that appears so often in Pompeii and Herculaneum wall paintings (particularly well-exemplified by the Pompeian room in the Metropolitan

*Red works well in dark rooms, where it lends an instant sense of warmth and well-being. Libraries, especially, benefit from a variety of rich red colors, as they create an even greater sense of the room being both a sanctuary and a retreat.*

*Combine reds of various shades—pinks, purples, and orangey browns. Then, mix the reds with greens and browns and touches of gold, as shown here, for a wonderfully cozy effect.*

Museum of Art in New York City). And what about sensual corals, the color of cooked lobsters or shrimp, or the brilliant orange-reds of Chinese lacquer, which glazed whole rooms in the early nineteenth-century Regency Period.

From all this it is possible to see that when people say they have an antipathy to a particular color, what they may really mean is that they dislike a particular shade or tone of that color. And this applies as much to red as to any other color.

Remember: Color is very subjective, but it is also very multilayered. If you think you don't like a color, think of it in depth and you will soon have to admit that it is a particular *shade* with which you do not feel comfortable, not the whole gamut. Also, you do not have to use that color excessively. Instead of using it on the walls, introduce it in a carpet or rugs, upholstered furniture, drapery, trim, picture frames, and so on. You will still obtain a cheerful effect.

Reds of various shades can be combined to great effect: red with pink; dark and light reds with fuschia pinks, eggplant, red, and orange; scarlet, claret, and Chinese or Cranberry red; corals with red- or orange-browns.

Red can also be used with other colors. It is a primary color, and its complement is green, a mixture of the two other primary colors, blue and yellow. This means that almost any shade of green will go with any shade of red, the brown-reds, or rose, as will many yellows and blues. Ox-blood, a rusty brown-red, looks good with jute or hessian and soft, dark indigo blue. Cherry red, or cerise, is a formal-looking color and is often used with a lot of gilt. Terra-cottas in various tones look wonderful with soft greens, blue-grays, and ivories. Soft, slightly yellowy, deep rose colors go extremely well with clear blues, creamy ivories, and greeny blues, as well as with old dark oak, chestnut, or pine furniture. And orange-red and coral look especially good with beiges, biscuits, blue and white, eggplant, French and Oriental porcelain, mahogany, gilt, and brass.

"SCARLET WILL RESCUE A DULL WHITE, CREAM OR BROWN ROOM FROM DULLNESS QUICKER THAN ANY OTHER COLOR. A LINE OF SCARLET AROUND THE PANELS AND ON THE MOLDINGS; SHADES OF THIS COLOR ON CUSHIONS; AND, OF COURSE, CURTAINS TIED BACK WITH IT—ALL THESE ARE USEFUL."

BRITISH MODERNIST DESIGNER BASIL IONIDES, WRITING IN 1926

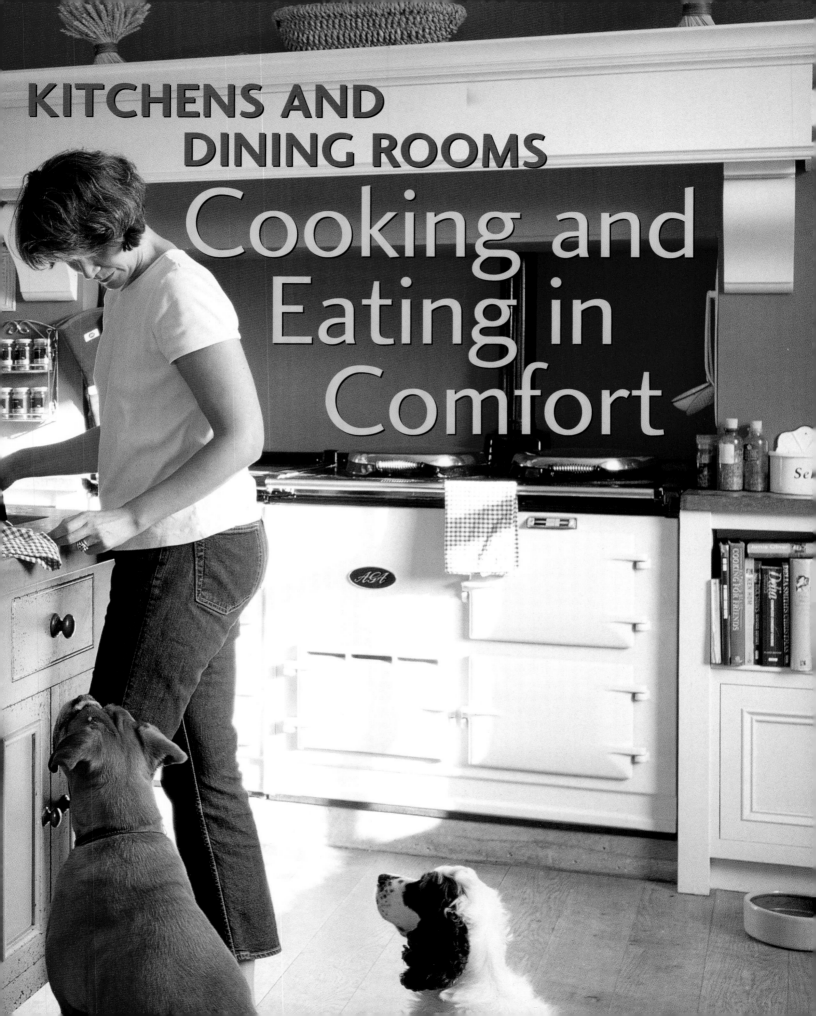

# KITCHENS AND DINING ROOMS

# Cooking and Eating in Comfort

*A happy, comfortable kitchen, or dining room, or dining-kitchen, filled with family and friends having a good time is a wonderful thing and definitely something to aspire to.*

There is something peculiarly ironic about current eating habits—with the take-out menus, "eat and run" dining, and meals eaten in front of the TV set—given the amount of time and money now spent on kitchen design and kitchen accoutrements, not to mention the huge sales of cookbooks, the equally huge audiences watching TV cooking shows, and the space given to stunning-looking kitchens in decorating magazines.

So are we to deduce that in spite of these hectic-life eating habits, deep down people want those days of entertaining, those simple, homey, family meals back again? Or are we all trying merely to satisfy our nostalgia in this vicarious way? Or—another thought—is it that we design and implement great cooking and eating spaces in the hopes that we *will* make use of them *someday* in the not-too-distant future—if and when we have time again? In other words, are all these beautiful and beautifully equipped cooking-living-eating spaces hostages, as it were, to fortune?

I prefer to think that because fashions in the design of homes, like so much else, are cyclical, and equally because so many of the old certainties have vanished,

FIFTY YEARS AGO, TO EAT IN THE KITCHEN WAS DEFINITELY DÉMODÉ. RIGHT NOW, GIVEN ADEQUATE SPACE, IT IS ONCE AGAIN THE NATURAL AND PRACTICAL THING TO DO. IF, THAT IS, YOU CAN GET EVERYONE TOGETHER AT THE SAME TIME. BUT AT LEAST THE SPIRIT IS THERE AND WILLING.

LEFT: *A beautifully laid table with matching linens, china, and flowers lifts the spirit and satisfies the soul. An attractive presentation will let your guests know that you want them to feel comfortable.*

OPPOSITE: *For centuries, kitchens have been the heart of the home, a space used for many functions in addition to cooking and eating. The sense of cheer and contentment that comes from the ritual of cooking and eating permeates the entire room.*

85

*Homey touches make a dining room and kitchen even more welcoming and embracing. Bowls of fresh fruit, jugs of flowers, bottles of wine, and containers of spices all lend to the ambience of the room.*

there is once again a basic yearning for that particular way of living, a need for stability and routine, even if it is mostly only possible on weekends. And I do believe that if we yearn for home comforts, every family should plan to have at least one proper lunch or dinner together on a particular set day at least once a week and have friends to dinner too as often as is feasible. Besides, most comfort food (and we are talking comfort here, are we not?) can be prepared in advance whenever there is a moment and stored in the freezer if necessary.

Today's eating mores, be as they may, really are an aberration in the big scheme of things. For centuries, at least for the so-called working classes, the kitchen was the heart of the house, and in many cases it was *the* room in every real sense the living room, used for almost every aspect of day-to-day life. So much happened around the kitchen fire: baking; spit-roasting (for those who could afford—or manage to poach—the meat, fowl, or game); salting and/or preserving vegetables and fruit; simple medicine-making with herbs; sewing, mending, spinning; eating; sleeping; births and deaths; and an occasional bath. True, the better-off kept their kitchens as far away as possible from the main reception rooms and bedrooms to avoid any residual cooking smells, and only very seldom visited them. Nevertheless, meals were planned and then appeared as night follows day, for labor was cheap and everyone who could afford it had at least one servant and a cook, and often quite a team, with an understood pecking order.

But all that changed after World War I, when each successive decade swelled the advance of the old domestics to the factory and the equivalent retreat of the mistress of the house to the kitchen (which, of course, was a far from popular swap).

By the late 1940s at the end of World War II, designers and developers had turned kitchens into smallish, streamlined boxes, and women, not wanting to be tied to the stove, welcomed them and their aseptic, clinical, easily cleanable, gleaming white enamel and laminate finishes. Kitchen unit and appliance manufacturers exploited the new female desire to get out of the kitchen as quickly as she could. In 1930 there were nineteen types of electrical appliances on the U.S. market. By the late 1960s there were around one hundred. Goodness knows how many there are today; currently, the choice of both appliances and kitchen units is immense, from slickly streamlined to nostalgic "farmhouse," from gleaming steel and tile to aged or painted wood. However, probably the biggest change is that it has been found practical in many family homes with small children either to design kitchens as large, open plan areas that accommodate living, dining, play, homework, desk, and cooking areas together (a throwback, of course, to the kitchen as *the* living area), or at least to combine cooking and eating areas. For very many people nowadays the kitchen area is truly the family room (while the living room, as mentioned in that chapter, is now, or should be, much more of a relaxing room).

In older houses partition walls frequently have been removed to turn dining and breakfast rooms into a larger space for a kitchen. Or the old kitchen and its attendant "still rooms" (rooms for keeping preserves), larders, storerooms, and so on, have been melded into one much larger space, just slightly separated by a counter, bar, or kitchen island. However, provided the kitchen itself is big enough, sometimes these kitchen-adjunct rooms are prized for their storage capabilities and the fact that there *is* a larder, that there *is* a special space for keeping jams, preserves, and so on. Others too turn them into small studies or play rooms, guest bathrooms, sleeping spaces for pet dogs and cats, or even home gyms. The point is that these adjunct rooms, whatever use they are put to, are indeed satellites, helping the main room, the kitchen, in its major role of servicing the home.

*It is common today to have large, open kitchen plans that combine cooking and dining areas with general living spaces. These adjunct spaces are prized for their extra storage capability, as the shelves in this dining area illustrate.*

# Creating a Well-Run Kitchen

The relevance, which is very often unconscious, of all the spatial and role changes made to today's kitchen is not only the practicality of being able to keep an eye on children when there is no help available, or being able to chat with family and friends while preparing and cooking food, but the fact that some of the warmth and bonhomie and comforting sense of ritual, which are—or should be—the inevitable by-products of cooking and eating, permeates the whole area. In many ways, in many peoples' minds, this atmosphere, if it can be achieved, is the distillation of home, what much of the feeling of "home" is about. The best kitchens for the way most of us live now are well-*used*, comfortable rooms that have the energy and atmosphere of a space used for many functions. And if the cook remains calm and unflurried, and can work comfortably and easily, the atmosphere will remain pleasant as well. But that requires planning.

## ORGANIZATION

The warm, heart-of-the-home feeling a kitchen may call to mind can be dissipated in no time by the detritus of meal preparation, scraps of food, and unwashed dishes, not to mention the tangles of toys and playthings. Here, as always, is where sensible organization comes to the fore.

### SURFACES

Clearly, a well-run kitchen has to work as efficiently and comfortably as possible. The surfaces of work tops, stove tops, appliance tops and fronts, splash backs, ventilation hoods, cabinet fronts, and walls should all be tough, durable, and, where appropriate, as seamless as possible so that they are easy to clean.

### STORAGE

*Storage areas should be carefully organized so things are easy to find and readily accessible. A collection of cooking pots can be tastefully hung from a wall, and dishes can be neatly arranged on floor-to-ceiling shelves.*

Maximum storage space is a plus. But efficiently and thoughtfully organized storage is the ideal. Here are some useful premises to follow. Deep drawers that pull all the way out (without coming *right* out) are best fitted with integral compartments to make the things stored there both better organized and easily accessible. Fitted knife drawers, for example, and sliding countertop chopping boards will allow for maximum economy of movement. Top eye-level cabinets should be deep too, with interior lights and glass fronts to enable the contents to be viewed immediately. This too avoids the unnecessary waste of time taken to root something out. Underneath these cabinets, install efficient recessed lights or concealed fluorescent tubes to cast an even light on the work surface below. Underneath these it might be handy to have long steel rods and hooks to hold cooking tools, canisters, spice racks, rolls of paper towels, foil and plastic wrap, sealable plastic bags, and anything else that is useful to keep close to hand.

## LABOR SAVING EQUIPMENT

The aim in a kitchen that is as much for eating in and for general day-to-day living as for cooking is to combine the most labor-saving equipment—self-cleaning ovens, freezers, large refrigerators, microwaves, waste disposal units, trash compactors, as well as generous work, storage, and dumping space—with what is perceived of as the warmth of the good old-fashioned country kitchen.

Many of the better kitchen equipment manufacturers produce what they call "workbenches," which are really work tops or countertops that incorporate cooking essentials such as cook tops, sinks, and waste disposal units as well as chopping and preparation space. The best workbenches contain all or most of the following elements: a length of deep countertop to keep cooking ingredients near to hand; a dual-power cook top with gas burners and/or electric halogen plates; a shallow sink for rinsing food and cleaning the cook and work tops; a deep sink for washing pots and pans; a movable chopping board that can be positioned next to the cook top; and a shute for a vegetable waste disposal unit. Top-of-the-line workbenches should be equipped to use both gas and electricity to take advantage of the strengths of each for various tasks (gas is better for simmering, for example) as well as to ensure that there is always one heat source that will work if there are power outages. They are also often free-standing, so that a couple of people—or more—can work comfortably at different tasks without getting in each other's way. Workbenches can, of course, be backed to a wall as well.

*Modern kitchen countertops often incorporate cook tops, sinks, and surfaces for food preparation. Chopping boards are also essential, as they can be moved from the sink to the preparation and cooking areas as needed.*

Try to provide the best waste and trash disposal that you can if it is too difficult to wash and clear up as you go along. A compactor is good since it can be slipped under a countertop, has a removable container, and reduces waste to less than a quarter of its original bulk. And try to ensure that there is as much dumping space as possible, which is mostly out of sight from the table.

If you would like to make a visual distinction between preparation and eating areas, you can change the floor between the two sections. In the sink and stove area, for example, use some sort of tile: terra-cotta, ceramic, flagstone, limestone, or comfortable cork and vinyl; for the area around the table, install wood floorboards. The table and chairs can top a large, washable area rug, or a division can be made with color—bright chairs, for example, or tied-on chair cushions and tablecloths. And, of course, a counter, or island unit, that can also act as a serving area will make a useful screen between cooking and eating areas.

## VENTILATION

Good ventilation is as essential in any working kitchen as good lighting. Cooking produces steam, smells, and grease-laden fumes, and condensation arises from the heat and moisture. Natural gas, if used, produces warm, moisture-laden air that condenses on contact with cold surfaces. It then becomes vapor, which spreads, leading to dampness and finally to spores. Condensation also causes wood to rot, plaster to crumble, wallpaper to peel, and a nasty black mold to grow. The best way to avoid all these problems is to extract water vapor at the source with a good ventilation system.

If you are going to eat and spend much time in a kitchen, a good ventilation system is also important because you will not want a steamy or smoky atmosphere, fumes, or unpleasant cooking smells. Though nice smells can all be mouth-watering and even somewhat comforting at the time, they are not nearly so attractive when they linger and grow stale.

There are several methods of ventilation from which you can choose.

- **Exhaust fans** expel steam, smoke, smells, and heat via steel or aluminum ducts or disused chimneys, either through the walls or the roof. They all are inhaled either by an external fan fixed onto an exterior wall, which is the most efficient, or by an internal fan mounted inside a hood. How well the system works depends upon the length and run of the duct system (short runs are better than long, circuitous ones), the power of the fan, and the placement and size of the hood.
- **Ventilation-grilles** are usually inset into a cook top with an internal fan that gulps up smoke, fumes, and odors before they have time to waft around the room, and vents them into the air outside. Such grilles are popular for island cook tops, but they are noisy. Also, they must overcome the fact that hot air rises.
- **Filtration systems** use changeable charcoal filters instead of ducts to filter smells and grease from dirty air, which is then refreshed and recirculated. These are really effective only in kitchens that don't see much cooking.

## The Question of Good Cooking Smells

Kitchens and dining rooms are the two rooms in the home where you will not want sweet-smelling things overshadowing or colliding with food smells (and that applies to flowers too). If, that is, the smells are as good as they should be.

But smells, like comfort in general, are very subjective. Some people love the smell of garlic and herbs and roasting meat or fowl. And there is no question (for those who love such things) that the smell of baking bread, or even the smell of frying bacon and eggs and coffee in the morning, is enough to get them leaping out of bed all bright-eyed and bushy tailed. Others absolutely abhor any sort of kitchen smells. Only trial and error will show you what is best for your own particular lifestyle. But bear in mind that the immediacy of delicious cooking smells is one thing. Stale cooking smells are quite another. So attend to that ventilation for long-lasting comfort in that direction.

Of course there is a wealth of kitchen deodorizers, plug-ins, plug-in oils, and so on available in supermarkets, but many people dislike their somewhat synthetic smells and think there is no substitute for fresh air.

OPPOSITE: *Good ventilation is an absolute must in a kitchen. A common method to achieve ventilation is to mount an internal exhaust fan inside a hood above the stove top.*

Always place light fittings in a position that is easy to get at. It is decidedly *not* comforting to have to get out a ladder every time you need to change a lightbulb.

ABOVE: *Kitchen curtains should be easy to clean in a color that blends or matches the wall color. Café curtains, shades, blinds, and shutters are all good choices for kitchen windows.*

OPPOSITE: *In kitchens, it is most desirable to have a bright light for food preparation, and a mellower light for dining. To efficiently yet gently light countertops, incandescent "architectural" tubes can be put under wall-hung cabinets, or behind baffles or concealing strips.*

### POSITIONING VENTILATION SYSTEMS

A ventilation system for a stove or cook top set into an island or peninsular requires more set-up work than one mounted against an exterior wall. The depth of the hood will determine how high it should be mounted. A hood that measures an average of 16 to 17 inches (40.6 to 43 cm) deep should be fixed 21 inches (53 cm) above the surface. But no hood should be mounted more than 30 inches (76 cm) above the work top.

Cabinet-mounted hoods should extend 3 inches (7.6 cm) past the cook top or range on either side. Retractable visors pull out to extract fumes and steam from the two front burners. Integrated retractable ventilators can be installed behind a hinged door or fascia panel so as not to disturb the pristine lines of an entirely built-in kitchen. Flat telescopic hoods, about 20 inches (51 cm) deep, slide out when required. Enclosed metal canopy hoods work well. And sometimes in older houses that have a chimney recess in the kitchen, a stove can be placed inside it to take advantage of the existing flu, thus negating the need for a ventilation fan.

## LIGHTING

You should plan for lighting that will highlight the table when necessary but not the sink or any uncleared messes. To achieve this, the ideal would be to put all ambient lights in the kitchen on dimmer switches so that you can turn the general lighting down as much as possible when eating (you will need *some* light for moving around), and to have separate switches for any fluorescent tubes over the work surface (their even light is excellent for food preparation) so that they can be turned off when not needed. Either a rise-and-fall lamp over the table or a down-light (again on a dimmer switch) recessed into the ceiling to hit the table center would be useful. And you will certainly need either a separately switched recessed down-light in the ceiling over the serving/carving area or a table lamp by its side.

## WINDOWS

Fabric designs and colors for kitchen window treatments should be kept simple. Good choices are straightforward checks or stripes or two-tone *toiles de Jouey* in an easily launderable cotton with perhaps a border in the wall color. Indeed, there is no point at all in elaborate window coverings in kitchen eating areas. They only get greasy, dirty, and in the way in an irritatingly short time. It is far better to use café (half) curtains, fabric shades, shutters, or blinds (but remember that slats get very greasy too, though at least they can be cleaned quickly). Fabric should be easily washed cotton, vinylized cotton (in the case of roller shades), or cleanable cotton (in the case of Roman shades). If windows are small, or tight up against a corner, inset shelves look good instead of any fabric treatment. They can be made of glass or wood, and used to hold collections of glass, this and that, or plants. Another suggestion is to just hang baskets of plants from hooks fixed in front of the windows.

# Choosing the Right Lightbulb

Although it is highly desirable to have as bright and unshad-owed a light as possible for food preparation (as well as for any bill paying, list writing, recipe studying, and homework done in the kitchen), it is just as necessary to have mellow light for eating. So for the sake of maximum eye comfort, it is important to understand the difference between the various kinds of bulbs available and what each can achieve. It sounds elementary to say that you should not buy light fittings for their looks but for what they can do for a room, but it needs to be repeated. And what the light fittings can do for a room depends very much on the bulbs with which they can be fitted. So here is a summary of different types of lightbulbs.

- **Fluorescent tubes** are certainly the most practical bulbs to buy and have lost most, if not all, of their residual reputa-tion for having a rather harsh light. They use only one fifth to one third of the energy used by incandescent bulbs of the same brightness, and have an average life of 10,000 hours or so compared to the latter's 750 to 1,000 hours. Equally, they now produce a diffuse, shadowless light that is excellent for food preparation, and they remain cool—an especially useful attribute in hot climates and hot kitchens alike. Although they *can* be dimmed, it is hard to do this without rather expensive equipment.

- **Ordinary standard incandescent bulbs** more nearly resemble daylight than flourescent tubes, and their warmth is flattering at night, especially when used in conjunction with a dimmer switch. However, they are more expensive than fluo-rescent tubes, are not so efficient in their use of energy, and do not have so long a life. They are best used in a kitchen in, say, pendant lights over a table, or in a three-way lamp, or pair of lamps, placed on a side or serving table and turned on at night when the cooking is done on late winter afternoons. You can also buy incandescent "architectural" tubes to put behind baffles or concealing strips of wood or metal, under wall-hung cabinets, and over countertops to provide an effi-cient but somewhat gentler light than the fluorescent variety.

- **Halogen bulbs** are not as energy-efficient as fluorescent, and rather more expensive. And they require literal kid glove treatment when being installed or replaced or they will be ruined. However, they consume around 50 percent less electricity than incandescent bulbs and last up to seven times longer. They also emit the brightest and whitest of light, and do not blacken like incandescent bulbs do. Because they are very small they can be used in much smaller fittings—those that may be recessed into ceilings, or soffits, or above and below shelves; they are also easy to use with dimmer switches for mood changes. Professional cooks' kitchens have for some time been using halogen bulbs with dichotic filters instead of aluminum ones to produce less heat, and these are becoming more widely available for the domestic market.

If you decide on either of these two last solutions and if the room is used for eating in at night, you might consider recessing a small, maneuverable eyeball spot in the lower edge of the architrave above the window to shine down on the shelves (especially if they are made of glass) or plants. Alternatively, if the window or windows are not too near a sink and the consequent risk of splashing the lightbulb or bulbs, you could think of recessing a similar spot or spots in the windowsill. If there is not sufficient recess space either above or below, or if the window surround is concrete, you could mount a small spot—or spots—attached to dimmer switches in the upper or lower corner or corners of the window. This will add extra dimension to the room, as indeed should any window treatment.

## COLORS

As in most rooms, the choice of color schemes for a kitchen are determined by location, size, quality of light, and climate as much as personal preference. Clearly an eat-in/general living kind of kitchen, especially if it's a good cook's kitchen, will require more thought than a streamlined, purely functional space, which is often better off just painted a good, clean white or a glazed, deep steel gray with white trim, offset with brighter accent colors in accessories and window coverings.

*White is always a good choice for kitchens. Combine the white with natural woods and bright accent colors in accessories and window coverings.*

I mention a good cook's kitchen because this presupposes that the cook cares about how food looks in the preparation as well as how it tastes, and there are certain wall colors that complement food more than others. Paramount in this category, I think, are the tawny colors from string and biscuit through to pale coffee, cinnamon, nutmeg toffee, and butterscotch. Some greens are good too, from grass and leaf greens to forest, hunter, and khaki.

These colors all look good with white or cream appliances and steel or natural woods, and can be sharpened with almost any accent color in accessories, window treatments, dishcloths, towels, storage jars, and so on. The tawny range also contrasts well with deep green appliances. Both color groups have the advantage of suiting any climate and can be tailored to different spaces and daylight allowance by choosing the lighter ends of the scale rather than the darker. Another advantage is that they all look as good in artificial light as in daylight and are pleasant to eat in at night, especially by candlelight.

A cheerful day-to-day kitchen color range that will help counteract less-than-generous daylight is buttermilk and the warm yellows, apricots, melons, and mangoes, again used with white. And if you like red, and do not have too large a space, scarlet can be a good wall color. In warmer climates, the blues—from sky blue through denim to darker blues—are cooling used, again, with white. Or, of course, white on its own.

## FLOORING AND WORKTOPS

If cooking is a major part of your kitchen life, you will usually need a floor that is comfortable to stand on for long periods of time. Unfortunately, comfortable floors are not necessarily the most handsome ones. For example, marble, slate, sealed and waxed concrete, and nonslip ceramic tiles might be fine for those whose excursions into the kitchen are mainly to forage in the refrigerator, put on the kettle, or collect glasses, cups and saucers, and tableware and cutlery for take-out food. But the hardness of these materials is undeniably rough on the back and feet, although many people are prepared to put up with the aches for the good looks. The French phrase *"il faut souffrir d'etre belle"* ("you must suffer in order to be beautiful") applies as much to surroundings as to the person, though washable rugs in the right places do help.

Happily, there are good compromises, just as there are people willing to sacrifice a little comfort underfoot to aesthetics, easier maintenance, longevity—or even fashion—all of which attributes can induce other sorts of comfort than the merely physical.

Since both floors and work tops often make use of the same materials or a mixture, here are some pros and cons of the various choices, in alphabetical order.

**Bricks** are heavy, so they are much more useful—and in any case more suitable—for a country kitchen floor than an urban one unless the kitchen is in a basement or on the ground floor of a house without a basement, although it still has more

*Colorful accent pieces will go a long way in adding decoration and charm to a functional kitchen. Dishes can be attractively displayed on open shelves, while collections of vintage kettles and pots can be showcased on side tables.*

Ceramic tiles are good-looking and practical on counter tops, work tops, and splash backs. Mosaic tiles can be arranged in brilliant patterns to make decorative yet durable countertops.

rural connotations. Note, though, that they might require extra support and should be well-sealed. Bricks are somewhat hard on the feet, but the color, especially of old bricks, is warm and welcoming. They age gracefully, and are easy to clean and maintain. They also lend themselves to some interesting patterns quite apart from herringbone and basket weave. However, because of their thickness, bricks are not suitable for work tops.

**Ceramic tiles** made from baked earth, clays, porcelain, or shale resist water and heat, last well, and are easy to clean and maintain. Nor do they need to be waxed or polished. They look clean and fresh in white or cream, which will, of course, go with any color in the rest of the kitchen. You can also make numerous designs using different accent colors and decorative motifs if you are so minded, and add in an odd old or handmade tile. Use special matching or blending nosing tiles for the fronts of the work tops, and trim tiles for finishing splash backs. However, nonslip ceramic tiles are hard on the feet, and most tableware or glass break on contact if dropped on them.

The three most used types are glazed tiles, quarry tiles, and ceramic mosaic. *Glazed tiles* can be glossy, matte, or textured, and if choosing them for floors, it is advisable to look for the type with slip-resistant glazes (spilled water or splashes can make the surface very slippery) or extra-duty glazes if the floor gets heavy traffic. Because of the variety of colors glazed tiles come in (including immaculate white), they can be juxtaposed in many different ways. *Quarry tiles*, which include Mexican tiles, are unglazed, with a natural clay color that develops a beguiling patina as the tiles age. Some quarry tiles are very soft and irregular, and others are very porous. You should definitely seal them before use with a penetrating oil to protect them from staining and again at regular periods thereafter to build up an immunity to stains. *Ceramic mosaic tiles* are very small, ranging in size from less than 6-inch to 12-inch (15- to 30.5-cm) squares. Mosaic tiles or terrazzo, a mixture of marble chips set in concrete, are good for decorative countertops. To stop sinks from seeping and leaking, use an insert variety with a sealed rim clamped over the top of the tiles, or overlay the edge of the sink with curved tiles.

If you use ceramic tiles for work or countertops and splash backs, make sure that you choose acid resistant porcelain or glazed tiles with a matte or textured finish and that you use a mildew- and stain-resistant grout with acrylic latex additives in a color that blends with the tile. The grout joint should be level with the tile and sealed or it will collect a lot of dirt. Make grout joints wider than usual for easier installation and cleaning. Use a waterproof grout sealant every six months and remove any stains that form in crevices with a small toothbrush. Other advantages are that they will not burn or stain and will withstand the heat of a saucepan full of hot water (but not a pan of fat). They look clean and fresh in white or cream, which will, of course, go with any color in the rest of the kitchen. You can also make numerous designs using different accent colors and decorative motifs if you are so minded, and add in an odd old or handmade tile. Use special matching or blending nosing tiles for the fronts of the work tops, and trim tiles for finishing off splash backs.

**Concrete**—that classic mixture of cement powder, sand, and water—is economical to lay and looks best in large tile form, and when waxed or stained and polished. If it is used in a kitchen it must always be sealed against food and oil stains. Concrete is currently very popular as a way of updating the look of older buildings and can also be used for work tops, if it is really well-sealed. Work tops can either be poured into forms on-site or measured and made off-site, then crated and shipped.

One disadvantage of concrete is that, if used as a floor, it is hard to stand on for long and it can crack and chip (although this last can be obviated with certain additives). Another disadvantage for people in a hurry is that it takes a good month for concrete to cure and become really hard.

**Cork** is certainly quiet and comfortable for the feet, light and easy to lay with glue, and develops a nice patina over the years. It comes only in natural colors and definitely needs sealing to prevent staining and to give it a longer life. The cork-and-vinyl variety is both durable and easy to clean, and although this latter is unusual for countertops it *could* be used there too as an interesting alternative. However, it would have to contain the vinyl content.

WHEN USING CERAMIC TILES, BUY MORE THAN YOU NEED AT POINT OF PURCHASE IF THEY ARE COLORED SO THAT YOU WILL HAVE SPARES FROM THE SAME DYE LOT IF ANY GET CRACKED.

*When choosing tiles for floors, look for ones with slip-resistant, extra-duty glazes that will withstand heavy foot traffic. Create simple designs combining white with an accent color, or by using a variety of colors that harmonize with the decorating scheme.*

*Warm yellow walls make a kitchen appear cheerful no matter the season. They go well with natural wood cabinets and dark marble countertops, as seen here. Seal the marble with at least two coats of varnish for added durability.*

**Flagstone** is actually bluestone or slate split into thin slabs. It was much used in old country houses and still looks good today. Flagstone can be sealed and waxed and polished, which makes for day-to-day easy maintenance (although it will have to be re-waxed and polished at periodic intervals), and it will last for generations. In its unsealed and unwaxed state it attracts a good deal of dust. Since, like brick, it is heavy, it is not suitable for urban houses, unless in a basement kitchen. Nor, like brick, is it suitable for work tops.

**Granite** is expensive, but it grows increasingly popular both as floor and work top material. Although it is in much the same price range as marble, and is just as luxurious, it is more durable, tougher, and more or less immune to stains and scratches as well as to fire. It is available in solid sheets or in thin tiles for easier laying, and comes in some fifty colors. A matte finish is less likely to be slippery, but a polished surface is extremely handsome and shows off the stone better. The flecked variety of granite is somewhat less expensive and perhaps a better foil for food. If used in a kitchen, it would be sensible to use the matte surface for the floor and the polished for the work or countertops. Although this combination would not make for a homey, farmhouse type of kitchen, it would be great in a hot climate, where cool is what counts for comfort. But a wood floor and granite countertops is a different story.

**Laminate and special countertop materials** are strictly for work or countertops, the former being very much less expensive than the latter. The former consists of thin, plastic laminate bonded to chipboard, plywood, or MDF (medium-density fiberboard) and can be installed flush to the walls and sinks. It is also easily contoured over rounded edges. It is affordable, easy to clean, easy to work with, reasonably heat- and scratch-proof, and comes in a huge choice of colors and designs. The disadvantages are that you cannot really chop on it, should you want to, and that it can chip, come unglued at corners, and peel if any moisture seeps through the joints. Nevertheless, it is enormously widely used.

Among the special newish countertop materials are Avonite, Corian, and Durcon, which are extremely practical but expensive. They are so solid that burns, scratches, and knife cuts can all be sanded out, and stains—even really bad ones such as those caused by nail polish, soft fruit and red wine—can be simply wiped away. This type of material can be cut, carved, and shaped like wood, and then molded into integral sinks and basins as well as used for draining boards, breakfast bars, and so on. The disadvantages are that it is heavy (Avonite is the lightest), it must be installed by approved installers so that perfect seaming is achieved, and it is not as handsome as natural materials.

**Limestone** is the epitome of cool. It looks wonderful on any floor in hot climates and can seamlessly proceed on outside to a terrace. It also looks handsome in cooler climates, either as a work or countertop or on the floor, combined with wood or butcher block. Like all stone, it is hard standing on it for a long time—but not that hard, given its looks. The polished variety can wear a little and get scratched, but it can be resurfaced. The etched or travertine variety is slip-resistant.

**Linoleum** used to be somewhat scorned as flooring and certainly could look dreary, stained, and shabby pretty quickly. Now, however, in its new form, it is comparatively inexpensive and comfortable to walk and stand on. And because it is lightweight, it can easily be cut and used for interesting inlays and designs. It should be sealed and is then easily maintained.

**Marble** is not your everyday kitchen or dining room floor material, but it is used a great deal for more upmarket urban kitchens and in hot climates. The A & B grades are tougher than the C & D varieties, but the latter are generally more decorative, though also more expensive. The downside of marble is that although it looks extremely luxurious, like many luxurious things it is a little frail and does not stand up well to wear and tear in a kitchen because it is both porous and quite soft. Also, it is slippery when wet (unless honed or otherwise treated), it is hard to stand around on, it stains and scratches, and it absolutely has to be treated with at least two coats of a penetrating sealer when it is first installed and then re-coated frequently thereafter. On the countertop side it is marvelous for

WORK OR COUNTERTOPS GET A LOT OF WEAR AND TEAR, EVEN IF THE WEAR PART IS JUST FROM THE OPENING OF BOTTLES AND THE SCRAPE OF ICE CUBE TRAYS AND THE TEAR FROM KNIVES CUTTING LEMONS AND AN ACCIDENTAL SCRAPE OF A CORKSCREW.

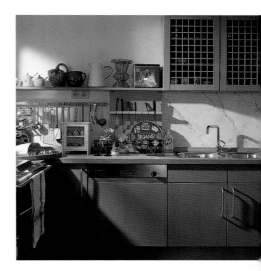

*Green cabinets and appliances contrast nicely with pale yellow or cream-colored walls. A smooth stone floor would look handsome in such a setting, but a nice, new linoleum may be a better choice for comfort.*

Stainless steel appliances and glass-fronted cabinets lend a hi-tech look to kitchens and dining areas. If desired, you can warm the scheme with natural wood and ceramic accents.

pastry rolling (and a slab of marble inserted into another surface such as butcher block especially for that purpose makes a lot of sense), but anything acidic such as wine, vinegar, or lemon juice, as well as sugar and alcohol, all cause it grief. If nothing but marble will do (and for some people, nothing else will), then I counsel choosing a dark color, honing the surface, and use at least two coats of sealant as for a floor. It is fine for a non-cook's kitchen or for anyone with a kitchen that is seen but not used or abused.

**Rubber** is certainly a comfortable choice for a floor, and industrial studded sheets or tiles have long been used in minimalistic and "hi-tech" kitchens. It also comes in a shiny finish like a wet suit, as well as in a wide variety of colors. It can be glued down on any firm, dry floor, with some sort of cap or metal edging for protection. Again, it does not provide your cozy, heart-of-the-home sort of look, but it is tough enough to withstand a wholesale family onslaught, and once again, it is really comfortable to stand around on.

**Stainless steel** is popular as a work top and back for its somewhat businesslike look and for the fact that it also mates well with a good many other rather warmer-looking materials. It is available in large sheets so that it can be used to form a whole countertop as well as a sink, draining board, and the surround for a cook top. It is also extremely hygienic, so is particularly useful for a young family kitchen. Buy the best quality you can afford because it wears better, rejects stains, and is excellent with heat. The bad thing about stainless steel is the way it gets marked and splashed and the fact that carbon steel implements like whisks and knives, if left standing on it for long periods, will cause rust marks. Counteract the spotting by using a fine abrasive cleaner, always in the direction of the grain, and use only cold water to wipe and rinse the surface—hot water leaves more spots. White wine vinegar is a miraculous grease spot remover for this material.

**Vinyl,** like linoleum, has reemerged with good new colors, interesting designs, and dead ringer imitations of all the best natural materials. It is reasonably priced, is truly cushioning for the feet, and is available either in wide sheets for seam-free fitting (at least in an average-sized room) or in tiles. It does, however, come in all sorts of qualities, so it is best to shop for it judiciously, bearing in mind that generally the thicker it is, the better. Cushioned sheet vinyl is probably the most comfortable; it is a little vulnerable to cuts from sharp objects, but that means that it is correspondingly easy to cut up and inlay into interesting designs. It is excellent for a young family room.

**Wood** is actually a marvelously versatile floor covering for both kitchens and dining rooms, especially now that the new generation of sealers and plastic finishes enables it to withstand staining, spills, and overflows of water. It is easy on the feet and easy on dropped china and glass. It is also warm-looking and practical for countertops if both top and bottom are protected by a coat of lacquer or an annual application of linseed oil-based sealant to prevent wear and tear from hot and cold water and general spillage. Butcher block turns a work top into one long chopping board, and oiled wood, because it has a matte surface to start with, tends to improve with age and is generally more resistant to heat rings than the lacquered variety.

*A long butcher block table sits at the center of this cozy, country style kitchen. Protect wood tables, countertops, and floors with a coat of lacquer or with annual applications of linseed oil-based sealant.*

# Creating a Beguiling Dining Room

ABOVE: *Traditionally, dining rooms are darkly colored, with heavy fabrics and ornate decorations.*

OPPOSITE: *The table should be gloriously illuminated with accent lights directed on paintings and other objects.*

Dining rooms, unless just off or open to the kitchen area, are far more inclined to be turned into more practical dual-purpose rooms, most commonly dining room-libraries, dining room-studies, dining room-conservatories, or even, occasionally, dining room-guest rooms—the dining function used only fairly occasionally for more formal or holiday occasions. But then, the dining room has never had the centuries-old tradition of the kitchen. Up until the eighteenth century there was no real room set aside just for eating purposes. Tables and chairs were set up and food was served in whatever room seemed most convenient. However, when a separate dining room became desirable, it was generally one of the biggest and best rooms in the house. It was also the most masculine.

The "masculinization" of the dining room arose from the Anglo-Saxon after-dinner habit calling for the women to leave the men to drink, smoke, and talk in the dining room while they repaired to the drawing room for tea and conversation.

The drawing room began to be regarded as feminine and the dining room mainly as the province of the men. This often resulted in heavy, dark decoration, especially during the nineteenth century, and the tradition still is to color the dining room richly.

The reason for this tradition may well have started, as Mark Girouard posits in *Life in the English Country House* (Yale University Press, 1978), when drinking tea and coffee became fashionable during the 1670s and 1680s. Both drinks were normally served after dinner or supper and were generally brewed by the hostess herself, who retired with her female guests to perform the ceremony. The women were joined by the men when all was pronounced ready. The interval gradually grew longer and longer, until it could last several hours, with the men drinking port and discussing politics and other subjects that at that time were considered more suitable for males.

## LIGHTING

Dining room lighting, as in kitchen-dining rooms, should mainly emphasize the table. This does not mean that guests will have to stumble around in the gloom before reaching their places, but rather that the table takes the central role at the appointed time. The most comfortable and flexible arrangement is to have adequate ambient light from valance or cornice lights, or up-lights or table lamps on side or serving tables, or (preferably recessed) ceiling spots and down-lights, or a mixture of all or most of these attached to separate dimmer switches. This is the ideal, for these separate dimmers will ensure that the main lighting can be turned down once diners are seated, while some of the other light fixtures can be adjusted to act as gentle accent lights to illuminate paintings, objects, window treatments, the side table, and maybe the table itself (which will preferably be candlelit, at least for a formal dinner).

*A pair of table lamps on a side table provide ambient light, while a chandelier shines from above the table itself. Fit table lamps with three-way bulbs so the light can be turned down for a soft and subtle atmosphere.*

Ceiling-recessed down-lights, suitably baffled to avoid glare, can be used over both side and dining tables with their level of illumination raised or lowered as required. If this is difficult, alternatives can be fitted: a rise-and-fall lamp, or a chandelier over the table itself and a table lamp or a pair of them on the side table. These too should be fitted with dimmer switches or, in the case of table lamps, at least with three-way bulbs. If accent light cannot be provided by recessed spots, up-lights in corners and angled spots placed on the floor by objects, windows, and so on will achieve much the same effect. In fact, I myself would always use floor-based up-lights and angled spots, whatever the other lighting.

## WINDOWS

Dining rooms and dual-purpose dining rooms (with the exception of kitchen-dining rooms, which should be treated as kitchens) can be fitted with whatever curtains or shades or shutters take your fancy, in much the same manner as living rooms and libraries. In fact, most dining rooms that aspire to a certain amount of nocturnal glamour benefit immensely from interesting curtains or draperies, especially if the room is lit mainly by candles (and better still, firelight as well).

A particularly good solution is to have permanently looped-back curtains with a contrast lining kept in place by brass or wood holdbacks, or by fabric or cord tiebacks, or maybe with a fixed heading and Italian stringing or reefing. (This is achieved by a diagonal line of brass rings and cords sewn into the back lining of the curtains, much as in theater curtains.) The window itself can then be covered with a shade, perhaps in the contrast lining, pulled down behind the curtains, to give a deeper, three-dimensional look. If the curtains are lit either by lights concealed behind a valance or by floor spots, the effect can be quite sumptuous.

## COLORS

Darker, rich colors are much better used both in regular dining rooms and in dual-purpose rooms, which are mainly used at night, than in day-to-day kitchens. Tones that may seem horribly dark and dreary at breakfast can seem quite glamorous at dinner, whatever the climate. The exception here would be conservatory-dining rooms.

Some good colors to choose for walls include Venetian red and crimson, glazed Chinese lacquer red, deep raspberry, terra-cotta, glazed Coca-Cola brown, umber, tobacco, nutmeg and cinnamon, dark greens, dark blues, and a deep apricot, and then picked up again in some measure in the curtains and tablecloth, if any, or perhaps in the napkins and tie-on chair cushions. *Complete* contrasts in the colors of the chosen window fabrics might break up the comforting continuity of dark and shadowed backgrounds against which food, fruit, and flowers, not to mention glass and silver, stand out or sparkle—especially in candlelight and subtle ambient and accent lighting.

## FLOORING

On the whole, hard floors softened by rugs are best in both proper dining rooms and dual-purpose rooms that encompass dining. This is mainly because carpet, however comfortable underfoot, is not particularly good at withstanding dropped food and spillage (although some of the synthetic fiber carpets such as the latest nylon and polypropylene are much more spillage/dirt resistant and harder-wearing than they used to be). Carpet also picks up and retains food smells and is inclined to become worn with the repetitive pushing in and out of chairs. On the other hand, hard floors can be clattery and noisy, especially when people push back and pull in their chairs.

There is no doubt that a centrally placed dining table on top of a large rug on a polished wood or stone floor of some type looks very good. On the other hand, there is the same problem with dropped food and spilled drinks as with a carpet. And generally speaking, the rug should be large enough so that diners maneuvering their chairs do not keep pulling it up. The comfort level here very much depends on the choice between aesthetics and practicality.

*Candlelight makes glass and silverware glitter and sparkle. Complement candlelight with subtle ambient and accent lighting to create a dining table that is stunning and memorable.*

# At the Table

## Comfort Zoning

### SEAT CUSHION BASICS

Make sure that seat cushions can be tied to the backs of chairs with ribbons of the same fabric or with the fabric of any binding or trim. It is irritating when they slip and slide, or keep falling off the seats when people get up.

*A round table invites conversation and conviviality. Arrange the seating to allow ample space for easy access and dining.*

## CHOOSING THE RIGHT TABLE

Kitchen and dining tables come in every sort of wood and other material, size, and shape—square, round, rectangular (refectory), and oval. Wood is undoubtedly the coziest material for a kitchen table. But when choosing a table, it is as well to bear in mind the space that each place setting will take up—if, that is, you are thinking of optimum comfort. Here are some facts to bear in mind when shopping:

- A round table is much easier for the placement of guests and for conversation.
- Each place setting with an armless chair takes up about 27 inches (68.5 cm).
- Add an extra 2 inches (5 cm) to this for chairs with arms.
- A long rectangular, or refectory, table should be at least 30 inches (76 cm) wide if both sides are to be used with comfort.
- Each person around a table will require a minimum of 30 inches (76 cm) to allow space for sitting down and getting up gracefully from a chair.
- Allow ample passageway around the table for people pushing back their chairs and for serving purposes. About 36 inches (91 cm) is really the minimum space needed.

## CHOOSING THE MOST COMFORTABLE CHAIRS

When buying a table and separate chairs, or when buying chairs for an existing table, or a table for existing chairs, try to spend some time sitting *in* the chairs *at* the table before you make a decision. If you are buying these items separately, it is obviously easier to take a chair to the table rather than the other way around. Most salespeople or antique dealers would be sympathetic to you borrowing a chair if you leave a deposit. If that is impossible for one reason or another, make sure you take along accurate measurements for the table height from the ground (taking into consideration any apron to the table that might hit knees) or seat height and width.

As with the choice of a table, here are some things that should help you in your selection of chairs:

- Make sure that chairs are a good height for the table—29 to 30 inches (73.6 to 76 cm) is the average height of the underside of the top of a table from the floor.
- It is wise to allow between 10 and 13 inches (24.4 and 33 cm) from a chair seat to the underside of the table.
- If space is limited, make sure that any chair with arms will fit under the table when not in use.
- If chairs are going to have cushions, remember that this will change the relation of the height of the seat from the underside of the tabletop.

## SETTING A COMFORTABLE TABLE

A well-laid table is always welcoming. And an interestingly or beautifully laid table certainly cheers the spirits—as does interestingly or beautifully presented food. I've always felt that the old expression that someone "keeps a good table" means much more than knowing that someone will always have an abundance of food and drink on hand. It also means, I think, that you can be assured that whenever you visit that home, there will not only be carefully chosen food with appropriate accompaniments, but that it will be well-presented and that this combination of good tastes and attractive presentation will add an extra dimension of well-being in a welcoming, gently lit room.

*A gently lit room, a beautifully laid table, and an abundance of food and drink . . . all of the ingredients of a welcoming, and comfortable, dining room.*

## Table-Setting

Among the things that I collect for table settings are candlesticks and candelabra; small, decorative glass night-lights (at night, in addition to centrally placed candles, I nearly always put a small, colored glass night-light in front of each place); small vases and interesting containers for flowers; and *low* porcelain planters for small plants.

All of these things mean that one can experiment a little with new juxtapositions and color combinations whenever one sets a table, whether it is an informal kitchen supper for two; a leisurely weekend breakfast (when bowls of whatever fruit happens to be in season, baskets of jams, and Greek or Bulgarian yogurt make their own decoration); a summer lunch or dinner on the terrace for eight; or a more formal holiday dinner in the dining room or library, with its flickering candle sconces on the walls, dimmed spots on books and paintings, and tablecloth of shimmering gold glinting and gleaming in the candlelight. (And talking of holiday or other festive lunches or dinners, it is very comforting to bring out certain ritual things for the occasion: family memorabilia or heirlooms, special silver pieces—things that have become a family tradition for special days.)

*Pillows can be stacked in corners to use as desired to bolster and soften seats and seat backs or to lift small children to table height. Low containers of small plants and flowers add color and freshness to individual settings.*

*Family memorabilia or heirlooms, like this needlepoint tea cozy, add a homey touch to special occasions. Shimmering gold cups and a vase bursting with tulips provide just the right finishing touches.*

*For a formal dinner, sterling silver candlesticks lend polish to an elegant silver and white setting. Holiday dinners are the best time to bring out old family silver and crystal pieces.*

One of the advantages of the disappearance of formality and rigid (as opposed to *pleasing*) traditions, is that people can now appreciate simple and informal food and tableware just as much as offerings on a more magnificent scale. You do not have to possess exquisitely embroidered and starched table linen, a full set of matching dinnerware, antique silver, and Waterford glasses in order to entertain. A bare wooden table with a bunch of white daisies or garden roses in a small jug in the middle, simple wine and water glasses, small wooden bowls of *fleur du sel* by each place, checkered napkins, and plain white or brown pottery plates will look just as good in its own way.

All the same, eye appeal, though not of course as important as taste, does stimulate the taste buds as well as feed visual appreciation, and to eat something that looks as good as it tastes, at a table that is pleasingly set, will be trebly enjoyable.

One of the easiest ways to dress up a table is with the table linens. Since I mostly eat in the kitchen, or outside on my terrace, and only occasionally in my library-dining room, I now have a whole cupboard full of tablecloths and napkins in numerous different colors and patterns, quite apart from my collection of over-sized antique white linen napkins. I bring out my various linens to suit the weather, or the food, or my mood, or the guests, or the occasion, whatever it happens to be. I also have a collection of various plates, serving dishes, and platters that I picked up from here and there over the years. I do not possess a full set of matching dinnerware, and never have. But I do have set upon different set of side plates, entrée plates, dinner plates, and dessert plates and compotes, so that every course can be differently served. (This is apart from my own design blue-and-white tableware, which I often serve on various blue-and-white tablecloths, with blue-and-white, or white, or blue napkins and a white jugful of delphiniums or lupins or cornflowers or forget-me-nots or whatever blue flowers happen to be in season.)

## FINISHING TOUCHES

The one thing every entertaining table has to have (and for that matter, every everyday table—why not?) is a centerpiece. This can range from a simple bowl of flowers, to a circle of small bud vases, to a low jardiniere of miniature box plants. Here are some ideas.

- a small ornamental birdcage full of apparently climbing flowers
- a compote from a dessert service, or a glass cake stand, piled with shiny red or green apples or tangerines
- a small basket or dish holding a pyramid of crystal balls
- one of the very many fanciful house- or temple-shaped bird feeders there are about, surrounded by scattered flowers in season
- a collection of miniature boxweed or bonsai trees
- the most stunning old candelabra you can pick up, surrounded by flowers
- a collection of different-sized candlesticks grouped together

Comfort Zoning
### ENTERTAINING BASICS

I know that people always mean to be helpful when they say, "Please don't go to any trouble when we come," but really, if you want people to feel comfortable when you entertain them, you *should* take the trouble and spend as much care on the presentation and the setting as on the food. It is just that you should not be *seen* to be taking trouble, because it embarrasses people and makes them feel uncomfortable. So you should try to organize entertaining meals when you have reasonably adequate time for the preparation. This is not to say that family meals should take short shrift; one should always try to set a pleasing table, but a table can be simple and casual without being sloppy. Just as busy people we learn to make effective shortcuts in almost everything we do, so too we can make shortcuts that work for cooking and for its appealing presentation.

# Whites and Neutrals

ABOVE: *Combine white walls with gleaming surfaces for a sleek and sophisticated look.*

RIGHT: *Enliven a white room with splashes of warm colors, like fresh pink, orange, and red flowers and fruits. Even the subtlest pattern or hint of color will stand out against an all-white backdrop.*

OPPOSITE: *Black and white is one of the oldest and most classic color combinations. An almost equally sharp contrast can be created substituting dark browns for black. White can also be used to enhance neutrals, like a beige or cream.*

WHITE-ON-WHITE-ON-WHITE is the epitome of cool. Of course it is the color (though white is not really a color as such) of snow. And white walls with gleaming terra-cotta or marble or patterned tiles on white are as much a part of hot climates as the sun itself. It was used to decorate houses both inside and out from earliest times. And today there are whole ranges of "dirty" or old whites, as well as blue-whites, creamy-whites, greeny-whites, pink-whites—whites with the merest tint of color, to accentuate and enliven surface variations and to give the subtlest of contrasts to moldings, trim, paneling, ceilings, and woodwork. This does not mean that whites and neutrals cannot be used with equal effect in cool and cold climates, but like blues and blue-greens, they will need to be sparked up with the odd flashes of warm colors, and the shine and shimmer of mirror, judicious lighting, candle, and firelight.

Any color you care to think of goes with white, including blacks (also not a color, but the sharpest contrast and one of the oldest of combinations) and deep browns (old black or dark-colored furniture, sparely spaced, will stand out like pieces of sculpture). A bright white will also freshen and enhance neutrals such as cream, parchment, ecru, taupe, stone, fawn, biscuit, beige, milky coffee, and khaki, or any of the various grays. In fact, a soft blue or lavender-gray with white is always one of the most comfortably, soothingly cool schemes in the heat, whether it is gray with white trim or white with gray trim. And the gamut of grays in a space, from the palest to the darkest, is decidedly restful.

# BEDROOMS
# A Tranquil Retreat

*The priority in any bedroom should surely be comfort—
not just comfortable for the body, but also comforting
for the spirit.*

A restful bedroom should include not just a comfortable bed and soft bed linens, but also subtly planned lighting, comfortable flooring, well-regulated temperatures, flexible ventilation, generous and well-organized storage, relaxing seating, and thoughtful window treatments that suit both partners if the room is shared. As an addendum to that physical comfort we also need to ensure maximum quiet and peace. This means that bedrooms in towns and cities should be rigorously sound-insulated with double glazing if necessary. Finally, you will want to decorate them as truly personal rooms.

Bedrooms are the most personal and private rooms in a home—the rooms in which we are supposed to replenish our psyches as much as our energy; the rooms in which we are meant to relax our bodies and our minds with regenerative and restful sleep. Given these indisputable facts, you might think that the *general* comfort of the room as well as the bed itself would always have been the priority in any but an ascetic's household. Yet the bedroom has had quite an extraordinary series of ups and downs; more so, really, than any other room.

Some of the most exotic and luxurious sleeping arrangements date back thousands of years, to the sumptuous bed chambers of ancient Egypt, Greece, Rome, and the Byzantine Empire. However, bedrooms deteriorated during the feudal societies of the European Middle Ages to the state where almost everyone slept hugger-mugger on the floor in one great room. Nor, except for monarchs and the most privileged of the aristocracy, was much regained of that ancient luxury or indeed privacy, at least until the seventeenth century.

Beds themselves fared no better. They veered disconcertingly from the sybaritic feather mattresses, silks and softest linens, wools and furs of the ancient world to the prickly sacks of straw of the medieval centuries. While the ancient beds were supported, as Homer and other classical poets and historians have attested, by frames of gold and silver, bronze and ivory, and precious inlaid woods, the medieval flea- and bug-ridden sacks of straw were dumped unceremoniously onto the unsavory hall floor of the local manor. At best, they were supported by benches to raise the lords and masters above the hoi polloi until the first "solars," or individual rooms, were added for the benefit of the landholders. These sacks eventually gave place to the wooden four-posters, which, together with their hangings, became the most prized item in most households.

Most beds of seventeenth-century American settlers were unadorned wooden boxes sporting, if lucky, a feather bed under a sheet and blanket. Some beds had

ABOVE AND OPPOSITE: *While beds in ancient Rome were supported on frames of gold, silver, and precious inlaid woods, by medieval times beds were reduced to simple sacks of straw. Today, the luxury of the past has been recaptured with stunning beds of every description and a huge choice of pillows in fabrics ranging from plain cotton to colorful silks and satins.*

# Comfort Zoning
## MATTRESS BASICS

Anyone buying a new mattress should spend some time lying on it in various positions, together with any partner. This is the only true way to test the comfort factor. If partners have different requirements from each other, as they very often do, those differences can be easily accommodated by having two different mattresses zipped together. If you have your heart set on a feather bed, remember that these mattresses, which are somewhat like feather-filled duvets, are meant to fit between a regular mattress and a fitted bottom sheet. So buy one that is slightly larger than your bed size—for example, if you have a queen-size regular mattress, buy a king-size feather mattress, and so on. (For sources, see page 174.)

*Around the early to mid nineteenth century, beds began to be looked upon once again as an important piece of furniture. The elegant simplicity of this antique bed combines beautifully with the white linens and neck roll pillow. In addition to antique beds, there are reproduction beds available that are indistinguishable from the originals.*

bases of solid boarding. The majority had cords stretched across the bed frame to support the mattress. The better ones had bases of sail cloth that was fixed to a roller at one end, tightened, and then held taut at the other end by a ratchet. Above this went one or two straw mattresses and, in more prosperous homes, a deep goose feather bed—layered like the bed of the tender princess disturbed by a pea. They were so high that householders bought steps (often used as bedside tables with lift up-lids for storage) to enable them to climb into bed.

The low "French" bedstead, based on the Empire sleigh bed, did not come into general use until around 1830. Although wooden bedsteads gradually gave way to iron and brass, most beds did not become as we know them now until later in the nineteenth century. The discomforting and perhaps little-known fact is that people did not stop complaining about bed bugs and fleas in their diaries and in household records until the regular grumbles tailed off after the Edwardian period at the beginning of the twentieth century.

And what of mattresses? Actually, it took a long time to replace the sacks of straw and their infinitely superior replacement, the feather mattresses. And some peculiar stuffings were used until the box-shaped hair mattress made an appearance in 1781, in spite of the fact that hair had, in fact, been used as an occasional filling from about 1650. Moss, for example, said to repel mice and other vermin, was used from 1770. Beech leaves were recommended as "remaining sweet and elastic for years." Pine shavings were advised in America in the 1880s to relieve bronchial troubles. The Irish were said to have used seaweed.

British patents for spring-coiled mattresses date to the eighteenth century, although the spiral spring was not really satisfactory since it tended to collapse on its side under any weight. The conical springs that replaced them were better, but they were subject to breaking and poked through their coverings to painful effect. Then came the woven-wire mattress, which had the reputation of being wonderfully comfortable until it started to sag. Today, the coil springs first thought up in the early nineteenth century have come into their own, packed in separate fabric cylinders to keep them well under control. But anyone who has slept night after night on a poor mattress, or a mattress that does not suit his or her physiognomy, knows only too well how important the right sort of mattress is, not just for a good night's sleep but also for the health of the spine.

Although the last millennium took such a painfully long time to catch up to some of the comforts of the ancient world, today we have a whole raft of accoutrements for the bedroom that not even the richest of all emperors could have possessed. There are stunning beds of every description, style, and period; beautiful bed linens; mattresses to suit every possible type of body and weight; a huge choice of pillows; sophisticated central heating and air conditioning to keep the temperature at optimum level; light that can be raised and lowered at the touch of a dimmer switch; electric blankets and pads; sumptuous carpets and rugs; excellent and flexible storage; and an extraordinary choice of fabrics, paints, and wall coverings.

*"Platform bed" is the name given to any bed whose base consists of a raised, flat horizontal surface. If desired, the space under the platform can be used for storage. The clean lines and sleek appearance of this platform bed would suit just about any bedroom décor.*

# Creating a Restful Bedroom

## STORAGE

Having enough space to comfortably house all your possessions with everything in its proper place is a comfort in itself. This is particularly true in a bedroom, which you would like to think of as a calm, uncluttered space. But before you plan bedroom storage or what you can do to extend the storage area you have, think first if there is any possibility at all of transforming a small nearby room, or even a landing space, into one large, beautifully planned walk-in closet or storage-dressing-room. This would be the ultimate in comfort. And you only have to make a list of the things you generally need to store in a bedroom or for your day-to-day dressing and maintenance needs to understand why this would be so. Once you start to write it down you will see that it is way longer than you probably ever imagined.

## FREE-STANDING STORAGE UNITS

If you do not have the space (or the funds) for separate, beautifully planned storage-dressing rooms, then whether storage has to be custom-built, bought ready-made,

*Free-standing chests, dressers, armoires, and wardrobe closets are all practical and attractive storage solutions for bedrooms. Here, a pair of natural pine armoires provides ample space to store clothing and bed linens.*

or somehow improvised, it usually makes sense to try to fit it into a bedroom as inconspicuously as possible. In a bedroom with high ceilings, beams, or nice moldings, it would probably be more in keeping with the style of the room to customize the interiors of old armoires, roomy old cupboards, or huge wardrobes that can often be picked up quite inexpensively from thrift and second-hand stores. Underclothes, sweaters, and so on can be kept in bureaus or dressers or chests of drawers. And if storage space is still at a premium, use chests of drawers on either side of a bed for bedside tables and a chest or trunk at the foot of a bed. You can also make window seats with lift-up lids, or a bank of drawers underneath. Any space under a bed can be used for luggage or shallow storage bins.

*Sweaters and clothing can be kept in bureaus or dressers or chests of drawers. If you have convenient recesses, drawers can be built right in the wall and matched along the front.*

## BUILT-IN CLOSETS

Bedroom storage has to take care of most, if not all, of our personal possessions and sometimes personal papers and records too. Therefore, for general comfort, closets and drawers must be considered as an essential part of the general design of the room. If you decide to have built-in storage (or built-in-*looking* storage, because most storage units are modular and can be made to look custom-built) and you have convenient recesses, or corners, or a whole spare wall, try to ensure

*Having an entire room designed to serve as a well-organized closet space is the most comfortable kind of storage there is. Yet many of us don't have this kind of luxury. Still, no matter the size of the space, it is important to have closets well-ordered, with bars to hang clothing, drawers for clothing, and racks or shelves for shoes and whatnot.*

## Comfort Zoning
### CLOSET ORGANIZER BASICS

The inside organization of closets is extremely important for the maintenance of order, the most efficient management of time, and therefore general comfort. It is no good having a neat exterior and a jumble of clothes and shoes inside. There are a number of specialist consultants who will organize efficient closet organization, as well as companies that specialize in providing logically thought-out closet interiors. And I reiterate that the most comfortable solution of all, if it is at all possible, is to designate a small room just for *well-organized* storage.

However, simple rules to follow if you are organizing the given space yourself include clothes bars attached high up for long and longer clothes, and lower bars for jackets, shirts, and skirts. Ideally, shoes should always be placed in racks or on shelves so that they are close at hand. Sweaters, scarves, and underclothes should either be neatly stashed in drawers (the former keep better in clear plastic bags) or stored in plastic containers or wire or shallow wicker baskets on shelves within the closets. Plastic containers or either wire or regular baskets can also be attached to sliders at the sides of bays or alcoves within cupboards to enable them to be pulled in and out easily. Deeper baskets can be placed at the bottoms of cupboards in shoeless spaces to hold all those bits and pieces that seem to defy normal categorizing, as can small filing cabinets for papers. Purses and bags should have shelves—or baskets—to themselves, as should any hats. Deep top cupboards are useful for storing suitcases and travel bags. Closet organizer containers in a variety of shapes and materials for different clothes and objects are available in most good stores.

that the closets reach ceiling height (usually with a row of cupboards at the top).
Also make sure that any preexisting moldings or baseboards that have been covered
in the process are reintroduced and matched along the fronts. Few things spoil the
proportions of a room so much as an unsightly gap between the top of a closet and
a ceiling, quite apart from the fact that it is an unnecessary waste of precious space
and a dust trap. If this makes the top cupboards very high, you can put your least-
used objects up there and reach them when necessary with a small step stool.

To be really unobtrusive, any sort of closet fronts should be made to seem part
of the walls and brought in with the same decorative treatment, whether painted,
wallpapered, or covered with fabric. Wallpaper or fabric should either be wrapped
around the doors or brought to the edge and finished with thin beading to prevent
frayed, torn, or worn edging. If you give wallpapered doors a coat or two of matte
or eggshell polyurethane, this will make them much tougher. Alternatively, some or
all closet doors could be mirrored (a good solution in a rather small or dark room,
where this will expand both space and light).

If, on the other hand, you want closets to look like objects in their own right,
they should still, if possible, incorporate some detail or feeling from the rest of
the room, whether it is in color, trim, general proportion, or just overall feeling.
For example, they could mirror the actual paneling of the doorway to the room,
or be fronted by handsome old doors that fit with the period or style of the room.
Or the panels alone could be painted or papered or covered to match the walls
or room fabrics.

## Conjuring Up Space for an Extra Closet

Sometimes you can look at a bedroom and think that there is no
place to put a closet. But look
again. A wall that has one or two
doors in it, for example, could
have closets built around the
door or doors. The same thing
could be done around a window
or windows, especially if you can
incorporate drawers or even a
dressing table and stool as well.

Occasionally in a smallish
room you can build closets
around the back of the bed space
with the top cabinets continuing
over the bed to form a recess.
Sometimes it is possible to fit
small shelves at the sides of the
cabinets to hold books and other
bedside items. Recessed down-
lights on dimmer switches can be
fitted to the undersides of the top
cabinets, or swing-arm lights can
be attached to the sides so that
everything looks integrated.

Also, you could put the bed
up against a window (as long as it
is well draft-proofed), leaving what
would have been the bed wall free
for closets. And, in a very small
room where there simply is not
space for closet doors, clothes
could be concealed by a curtain
that matches the wall finish.

ABOVE: *Closet organizers can help make
life easier and can actually double the
amount of storage in a closet. You can
customize your closet with shelves,
hanging rods, and drawers. There are
even drawer dividers that can further
help you to get organized.*

### ELECTRICAL OUTLETS BASICS

Before embarking on any bedroom renovations, make sure there are enough electrical outlets by the bed to encompass electric blankets or pads, an electric clock or clock radio/CD player, and any bedside lamps. You might also want an outlet somewhere for an electric kettle or tea or coffee maker, and of course for a television set, VCR, and possibly even a DVD. If you have a sink or dressing table, it is a good idea to have an outlet nearby for an adjustable magnifying mirror with an integral light and any lamps you position there, as well as for an electric shaver and a hair dryer.

## LIGHTING

As in most rooms, bedroom light has to be a mixture of good, overall ambient light and work—or rather leisure reading—accent light, as well as light for the insides of closets. Most make-up and shaving activities take place in bathrooms, but if they take place at a dressing table or sink in the bedroom, these areas will have to be appropriately lit as well.

Recessed ceiling lights seem to me to be a distraction in a bedroom, unless they are exceptionally small and neat and are subtly distributed. There is a generous choice of charming ceiling fixtures (to suit every possible taste and pocket) to provide ambient light, or it can be provided by lamps. If you do use lamps, at least one of them (and preferably all) should switch on by the door and off by the bed and be attached to dimmer switches, or at least three-way bulbs.

Good bedside lights are incredibly important for comfortable reading in bed, yet they are so seldom carefully chosen. All too often they are so small that you have to lie in an uncomfortably scrunched position in order to see properly. Or their wattages are too low to provide sufficient light to read by. Swing-arm wall lamps with integral dimmer switches fixed at an appropriate height slightly to the right of the pillow are always successful. But if you choose table lamps, select them first for their height and second for their looks. The light should shine *down* across your shoulders, onto the pages of your book.

It is as infuriating not to be able to see clothes properly inside a closet as it is not to see the pages in a book, so make sure that there is internal lighting when the closet doors are opened, or at least a good light just outside them. Since there are no actual "closet lights" available, use regular strip lights or a small bracket light. Ask your contractor to provide the kind of switch that automatically switches on and off with the opening and closing of the doors.

*Bedside lights should be tall enough that you can sit comfortably in the bed while reading. The light should have adequate wattage to read by, and ideally should have the capability to be switched on near the door.*

If you have a sink or dressing table in the bedroom, both shaving and make-up light should be as bright and unshadowed as possible. "Hollywood" strips on either side or, if necessary, on top of a fixed mirror are excellent, but try to have them on a dimmer switch if they are not separately switched. Also, have good lamps on either side of a dressing-table mirror. A designer I know always specified that the shades on dressing-table lamps should have a gap at the top so that the shades could be twisted around when necessary to have the benefit of the bare bulbs and twisted back to look normal when not in use.

## WINDOWS

Few of us can boast beautiful bedroom windows, which ironically is just as well since it would be a crime to cover up a really gracefully shaped and framed window—and most often bedroom windows do need covering, unless you can install a shade within the reveal that will still show off the handsome shape. In the case of arched windows, there are now flexible rods for sale that can be bent to the arch shape. Happily, the average room possesses pretty standard sash or casement windows that take well to shutters or, for a softer look, headed and tied-back or held-back curtains used in conjunction with sheers or shades, whether custom-made fabric or one of the many, many different choices of ready-made louvered or mini blinds. But quite often windows are just different enough to be awkward and to

*Floor-length curtains can be tied back and combined with sheers or shades for a soft and elegant look. If desired, fabric curtains can be matched to the wall covering and bed linens for added refinement.*

# Controlling Light through Windows

Rather like in the choice of mattresses, different people prefer quite different levels of daylight. Some love to wake up with light streaming into the room, and find that this sort of natural awakening leaves them feeling refreshed and energetic after their night's sleep. In fact, some cultures have made a point of placing their beds to point to the East. Some early twentieth-century cribs actually have built-in compasses to set them right. (Feng shui followers, of course, would insist that whatever its orientation, the bed should be placed with its head to the wall so that occupants can see anyone coming into the room.) Others could not care a toss about such theories and do not want the merest sliver of light to filter in. For couples who have these different sensitivities to light, the choice is hard. One or the other has to give in and learn to love the alternative way, come what may. It is my observation that it is generally the light hater who seems to win. To please him or her, the most fail-safe way is to have a shade made that is lined and interlined with blackout material, plus floor-length curtains that are also lined and interlined. If you only want a shade of some sort, then you should try to ensure that it is hung so the edges are outside the window frame, or that there is a wide and deep slit carved into the sides of the window frame into which the sides of the shade can be slotted and then pulled down so as to avoid light spilling out the sides. But even with the best will and the cleverest curtain and shade maker in the world, you will not be entirely light-proof if you set shades inside a window embrasure. A good compromise is to hang the aforementioned blackout shade, and then have curtains that meet in the middle and are permanently caught back at the sides to block out the light from the edges of the shade. You could buy a four-poster bed with curtains that could be drawn at night if you are not a fresh-air enthusiast.

And that is another thing: those who like windows open at night and those that do not. Again harsh choices have to be made.

LEFT: *A good solution for controlling window light is to install a black-out shade behind floor-length curtains. The curtains can then be permanently caught at the sides, which would shield light from the edges of the shade, or occasionally loosened to meet at the middle.*

cause problems when it comes to covering them (especially true of pivot windows or the long, shallow "ranch" or clerestory windows and their antithesis, whole walls of glass or a series of French windows so beloved by property developers in the southern United States—and so complained about by their subsequent owners).

Nevertheless, there are solutions to "problem" windows. In the case of pivot windows, casement curtains fixed right against the glass and secured at the top and bottom by expandable spring-pressure curtain rods—slipped through narrow casings stitched into the fabric—is probably the best solution.

Ranch or clerestory windows need shades of some description. Those fixed above the window frame and made to drop well below the sill are best, because they would look odd and out of proportion when lowered if made to cover the window exactly. In the case of walls of glass or large picture windows, where curtains might look rather fussy, you will be best off with a series of shutters, or Japanese Shoji screens, or Roman shades, or vertical louvers. French doors that open inward work quite well with curtains attached to a nineteenth-century-style *portiere* rod, one end of which is fixed to the door frame and the other to the far side of the door. The rod swivels so that the curtain or drapery opens with the door.

## COLORS

Bedroom colors should, on the whole, be restful, such as blues and whites, ecru and white, rose and cream, grays and whites, or pale gray and white. If you want more accent colors, such as deep lacquer reds, greens, and apricots, add them with trim, cushions, throws, lamp bases, art, photograph frames, rugs, and so on, or even with the books in a bookcase. Of course, there are some people who prefer having strong, dark colors, and since bedrooms by their nature have to be really personal rooms, that is fine too.

In any event, much depends on climate, situation, and the view out of the window as well. A very green view, for example, can be charmingly matched by a variety of greens and whites and creams. Rooms with hot blue skies outside look cool and elegant in various blues and whites. Gray skies are always cheered by rose and cream schemes, or even dark tobacco browns and creams, with some red and beige accents.

## A FINAL THOUGHT

Since it is somewhat essential that bedrooms, above all other rooms, should be soothing rooms, my own thought is that whether they are for the full-time occupants of the home or for visitors, they should not be too smart or "designery." To my mind, they need to be gently and restfully eclectic and full of interesting memorabilia—rather than in any way grand or overdone—with an unforced sort of elegance.

Bedrooms—and I stress that this is only my opinion—need to look as if they have just evolved rather than look newly decorated, even if they are. I like them, in short, to be comfortable but vaguely haphazard sorts of rooms.

*Choose restful colors for bedrooms, such as blue and white, lilac and cream. Accent colors, like red, green, brown and black, can be introduced by way of fabric furnishings and decorations.*

# Guest Rooms

## Comfort Zoning

### GUEST ROOM BASICS

It is always a good idea to try out guest bedrooms from time to time. Only in that way can you find out if mattresses and pillows are still comfortable, if lightbulbs and other electrical appliances are all in good working order, and what flaws and missing objects there are.

To give pleasure to your overnight visitors, guest rooms should be made as comfortable, beguiling, and welcoming as your taste and budget allow. Clearly, it would be gratifying to be able to provide the most beautiful furniture and furnishings, rugs, paintings, and prints for your visitors, but since that possibility is somewhat rare, it is best to concentrate on providing creature comforts and at least interesting decoration. If your guest room has the luxury of a fireplace in it, you can have a fire gently flickering in the grate for the arrival of winter guests. Similarly, if the guest room has an adjacent terrace that is well-planted and private—ideal qualities for sunbathing—summer guests will think themselves equally blessed. If you cannot provide a fire, make sure winter rooms are well-heated. And if you do not possess air-conditioning, provide summer guests with good fans.

Obviously, you cannot hope to provide a mattress or mattresses that will suit all backs, but you can provide a choice of pillows from softest goose down to firmer synthetic filling (for those who have allergies to feathers), with a choice of neck and baby pillows as well. Sheets should be the best you possess.

Guest rooms should have good reading as well as general light and one of those tiny plug-in night-lights for those unfamiliar with the layout at night. Bedside tables should be generously sized, and there should be a comfortable chair or chairs, or a chair and a chaise or daybed with a throw. A full-length mirror is preferable, but if there is no room for one, try to place one on a wall of the landing or corridor outside. Provide plenty of drawer and closet space, with nice-looking clothes hangers and a space to stow suitcases. A well-chosen and appropriate pile of books and magazines and a nightly supply of fresh mineral water in a cooler are always welcomed. Nor should you forget to provide an alarm clock, a waste-basket, and small vases of fresh flowers or plants in attractive flowerpots.

RIGHT: *It is nice to supply a guest room with a choice of pillows ranging from the softest soft to quite firm. In addition, there should be at least one good reading light, and an extra chair is always nice.*

OPPOSITE TOP: *If there is a writing table or desk, consider providing paper and envelopes, pens and pencils for your guests' convenience. A generous selection of reading materials will make the room even more pleasurable for visitors.*

It is always a pleasure to find a writing table or small desk and chair in a room, even if the writing table doubles as a dressing table. And better still to find writing paper and envelopes, postcards, pens, a notepad, and even a sewing kit for odd repairs in a drawer. Nowadays too guests might appreciate an extra phone line and electrical outlet near such a desk for laptops, as well as a discreet TV.

If there is a discreet corner in the room where you can put an electric kettle, tea bags, sugar, tea cups, teaspoons, and saucers, as well as coolers for milk and even a hot water bottle for unexpected cooler nights, so much the better. And it is always a good idea to keep a supply of new toothbrushes, toothpaste, electric razors, regular razors, brushes and combs, and clothes brushes for guests who have forgotten to pack such items. These are all councils of perfection, although none are too difficult to achieve.

However, it is usually the actual furnishings that are more difficult to get together once the rest of the home has been furnished. Guest rooms are all too often filled with a mishmash of leftovers. Still, that is not nearly as much of a problem as one might imagine if all the furniture is given a coat of black or white paint, say, or even some distressed finish or other, and the upholstery, chair cushions, bedspread and skirt, window shades, and curtains are all either the same fabric or at least work well together. This way, the room will look all of a piece.

*It is thoughtful to welcome guests to your home with a serving tray filled with teapot, tea bags, spoons, cups, saucers, cream, and sugar. A small vase of fresh flowers will make the presentation even more graceful.*

BLUE IS ANOTHER receding cool color, and blue and white, in whatever weight or depth, is a much-loved combination in hot climates, as much for decorative schemes as for porcelain and ceramics. However, with the adjuncts of firelight, candles, good lighting, the sparkle of mirror and gilt, and perhaps a flash of some sort of red, blues and blue-greens are just as attractive in cooler climates as well. Equally, the darker blues and apricots and gold of Japanese Imari porcelain of the early eighteenth century, or the turquoise and eggplant of the Chinese Kang H'si period at the turn of the seventeenth century, or the magnificent blue and orange tiles of the thirteenth-century Moorish Palace of the Alhambra in Granada, southern Spain, could all provide ideas. It is also worth examining the wares of any good oriental carpet store. Look, for example, at the powder blue and contrasting pinky beiges, dark blues, and Indian reds of Kashan and Hamadan rugs from Iran; the beautiful creams and turquoises particular to the Middle Eastern city of Qum, or the dark blues and reds in Turkish rugs. A more homely but

equally cool color scheme could be inspired by blueberries and cream, or the pinky blue resulting from blackberries squashed into thick cream.

Theoretically, blue-greens could be described as brilliant turquoise at one end of the spectrum and limpid aquamarine at the other, with many variations in between. As a child, I was often told that "Blue with green should never be seen." The fact is, however, that almost any blue-green and blues *with* green are not only the colors of sun-lit sky, sea, grass, and trees—the most natural of combinations—but also among some of the most ancient of color juxtapositions. These colors figure prominently in the ceramics, rugs, and decorative objects of Peru, Tibet, China, Egypt, and Iran/Persia.

George Washington's house in Virginia, Mount Vernon, uses a strong turquoise against white. And I have seen other hallways in hot climates with pale turquoise or aquamarine walls and soft periwinkle blue doors and woodwork, as well as aquamarine used with grassy green and darker soft Prussian blue. But then, pale turquoise or aquamarine with white are peaceful colors for bedrooms and bathrooms too.

ABOVE: *This room, with its pristine white walls and gauzy white curtains, with touches of blue in the bed covering, headboard, and lampshades, would be a refreshing retreat on a hot and humid day.*

OPPOSITE: *Soft blue combined with white, cream, or pale yellow makes for a cool yet soothing color scheme and is especially well suited for bedrooms or guest rooms, where relaxation is of the utmost importance.*

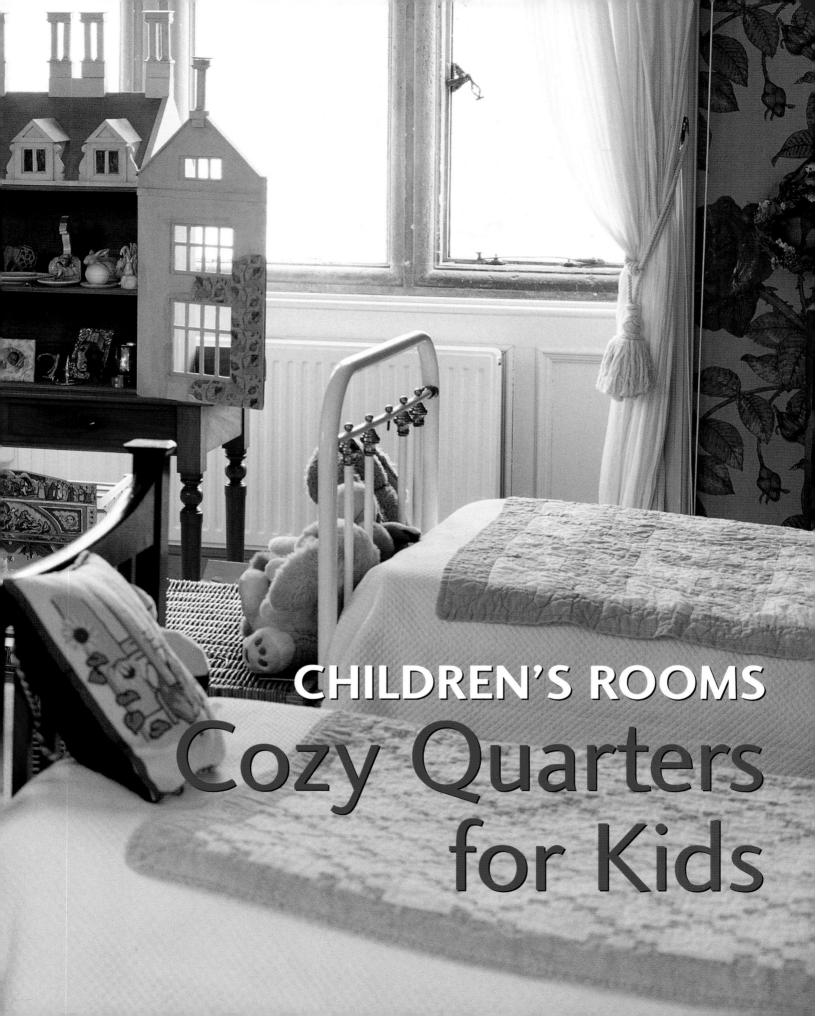

# CHILDREN'S ROOMS
# Cozy Quarters for Kids

*Since early experiences are formative, and since first memories stay with most people throughout their lives, it is only logical that children's room should be made as comfortable, comforting, and stimulating as possible.*

This certainly does not mean that parents should go over the top decorationally speaking, but rather that surroundings should be cheerful, practical, sturdy, and above all *safe*. It means that most furniture and furnishings should be designed, wherever possible, to last through childhood with only minimum modifications. It means too that lighting should be planned with thought both for infant needs and for growing children, that surfaces should be easy to clean, and that the chosen flooring should be as sound-absorbent as possible, for everyone's comfort.

All too often aspiring new parents think of a child's comfort in terms of luxury and being able to provide the latest consumer goods, which is so much the opposite of what should be provided. Think rather of all the other wider connotations of what constitutes comfort for a child. Providing a constant loving warmth, for example, with easy access to you as parents, but also a firm sense of right and wrong. Respecting your children's need for privacy as and when it is desired, but not leaving them wholly to their own devices. Ensuring that there is a proper home to which they can bring their friends, knowing that they will be welcomed. Providing firm parameters within which they can flourish and develop to feel comfortable in their own skins and with their own ideas and opinions. And above all, a sense of security.

ABOVE: *Whimsical accents, like these colorful figures, will add to the charm and magic of a child's room.*

BELOW LEFT: *Children's rooms should be warm and welcoming, with fabrics and furnishings that are practical yet cheerful.*

OPPOSITE: *A girl's bedroom is one of the best rooms in the house to decorate, and if you plan carefully it should have long-term appeal. A flower garden, whether rendered in paint or on wallpaper, is wonderful for a child as well as a teen.*

# Creating a Snug Children's Room

*The careless days of childhood need not mean a messy, chaotic room. Shelves and cupboards with lots of niches, baskets and boxes, and lots of hooks help keep clothes and playthings neat and tidy.*

It is interesting how many first-time parents, consciously or unconsciously, try to recreate, at least in some measure, the feeling of Victorian and Edwardian nurseries, with charmingly dressed cribs, a plethora of whimsical mobiles, a rocking chair or nursing chair, and a comfortable, battered old sofa. They would, I am sure, give anything to have a fireplace with a perpetually glowing fire. All that was literally a hundred years ago, but for many the term "nursery" still conjures up such a vision.

The fact is, though, that spending a lot of money on furniture and accoutrements for the first year or so of a child's life is more a gratification for the parents than for a child whose basic needs are to be held and comfortingly hugged, fed when necessary, kept clean and dry in an even temperature; to have a good, quiet, safe crib in which to sleep, a comfortable rug on which to lie, and as they become more mobile, a safe terrain to explore. Most equipment for infants (apart from the crib, baby linen, a consistently adequate supply of diapers, diaper wipes, soothing creams, bottles, and bottle warmers if necessary) is more for the comfort of the parents than the baby. Certainly, it is useful to have reasonable storage space for baby clothes (although drawers and a few hooks are perfectly adequate for some time), a comfortably supportive chair in which to nurse and feed a baby, a safe surface on which to change a baby, and possibly a maneuverable cart of some kind near the chair to keep a supply of all the daily grooming necessities at hand.

## PLANNING FOR THE FUTURE

As your family and your children grow, you will have to decide—depending upon the space at your disposal—whether their rooms have to become combined sleeping-cum-playrooms (which is the norm) or just bedrooms with a separate playroom (which is a luxury). Either way, it is both more practical and easier on the pocket if you can plan for, or make allowances when you are planning the space for, the kind of room that will grow along with the child. Try to keep in mind the subtle modifications you can make over the years so that with the minimum of background change, and thus expense, cribs can give way to cots and cots to beds, and toy and infant clothes cupboards to full-length closets and adequate storage for what is often the huge volume of teenage paraphernalia.

This does not mean that you or, when they get older, your children cannot ever go to town on the decoration. On the contrary. You—or they—can be as bold as you like with accessories, art work, fabrics, storage boxes, and so on.

What I stress is that the background or framework of the room should be planned to be as simple, sturdy, and classic as possible. In this way you can change elements such as window treatments, bed sizes, floor coverings, borders, wall hangings, and so on, as and when you need or can afford to without having to make expensive alterations to walls, storage units, and other basics. In fact, with a little ingenuity it is quite possible to make the same space work well and in different ways for years, even if newer children have to be accommodated there as well. After all, as generous an amount of storage as possible; a bed or beds or bunk beds (especially the kind which can later be made to look like a sofa or sofas), and if there is room, a spare bed, a sofa bed, or a bed that looks like a sofa for friends; and a worktable or desk or desks and chairs are all quite adequate basic furnishings. All the other ingredients—TV, stereo, computer, printer, throws, floor cushions, and pillows—you name it—can be added when convenient.

## SAFETY

When children are small, make sure that all of the following points are followed (and then some), and be ultra-careful. You may think you have everything covered, but it is quite extraordinary what children can think up to do, most particularly in the way of climbing up things you would never imagine they could and then gaily launching themselves off.

- Try to ensure that electrical outlets are flush with the walls and not placed low on baseboards or within crawling reach. If you can fit covers over unused outlets, so much the better.
- Keep all electrical appliances well out of reach and see that cords or wires are kept as short as possible so that they are not tripped over or easily pullable. Lamps should be placed so that they cannot be pulled over.

## Comfort Zoning
### SHARED ROOM BASICS

If pre-teenage children have to share a room, which actually many of them like to do, try to give each of them some sort of private or at least personal space in the room. Bunk beds with their own drawers underneath are one possibility; a low partition is another; or you could consider hanging a mosquito net over a bed or using a curtain of voile as a divider to give at least the *illusion* of privacy. Bookshelves, too, can double as room dividers.

*If the framework of the room is simple and classic it can be kept for many years, with only simple changes in curtains, flooring, and so forth, as the child matures. Over time, bunk beds like this one can be dismantled and made into single beds or even sofas.*

- Have nonslip floors, or as nonslip as possible. Tough, easy-to-clean carpeting is good in apartments or on upper floors of houses, because it is not only comfortable for crawling on but helps to deaden the sound. But see that the carpeting is smooth enough to operate wheeled toys easily.
- Make sure that any fireplaces, stoves, fans, and electric space heaters are well-guarded.
- Put safety gates on any flights of stairs and make sure that they are kept shut at all times and as a matter of course when toddlers are around.
- If children's rooms are above the first floor in a building, either fit window locks or temporary vertical bars to prevent kids from climbing out. Bars should be no more than 5 inches (12.7 cm) apart, but certainly not wide enough for a child to get his or her head stuck in or through. They can be painted in alternate colors or a mixture of colors to stop them from looking prison-like.

*Roman shades are ideal in children's rooms, and can be hung outside the window frame to block out the morning light. Windows can also be shuttered or fitted with roller shades.*

- Children love to climb and are often fearless about jumping off the object climbed. Although it is good to encourage self-confidence, self-motivation, and imagination, try to ensure that no surface is high enough to be a potential source of danger in a small child's room. And make sure that if he or she does fall, the floor is comparatively soft and there are no hard, sharp objects or corners of furniture anywhere near beds or bunk beds. Finally, check that drawers cannot easily be pulled out to act as steps (or be pulled right out for that matter).

- See that at least one light is on a dimmer switch so that it can be dimmed down to act as a night-light for children frightened of the dark. The same applies to lights in the hall or corridor outside. A dimmed-down light is also useful if you have a baby or babies that need to be attended to during the night without disturbing an older child. If you feel strongly about keeping lights on in the bedroom, however dimmed, and a child is frightened of the dark, buy a night-light or a small illuminated plug that fits into a wall outlet and gives a comfortable glow for almost no cost. And keep lights dimmed well down outside the room as well.

## LIGHTING

The safest and most efficient providers of ambient or general light in an infant's room that is to be both sleeping and play room are either pendant ceiling lights or glare-free recessed ceiling down-lights, placed over changing areas, the crib, the chests of drawers or bureau; or equally well-placed wall lights; or a mixture—but all of them attached to separate dimmer switches. In fact, the most comfortable way to plan the lighting, if at all feasible, is to install two-way switches with a separate switch where the future bed will be placed. This kind of planning obviates any safety hazards with table lamps and electric wires or cords that can be interfered with once the child starts to crawl, and allows for the light or lights to be dimmed for minimum disturbance during night feeds, as well as maximum reassurance during the night. Alternatively, that same night reassurance can be provided by one of the tiny night-lights that fit right into an outlet.

If you happen to be rewiring the room or installing more outlets, it would be forward-thinking to place outlets by the future desk or play/work station and near where a potential TV, stereo, or computer could be placed, as well as behind the future bed for use with an adjustable wall light or bedside lamp. For maximum flexibility I would also install pairs of outlets flush to the wall in corners (these will come in handy for adolescents or want to jazz up their rooms for entertaining with up-lights with colored filters). Think too of telephone jacks already in position for future Internet and telephone activities; it will save on both money and disturbance later. (Remember that all outlets within reach of a crawling child or toddler should be covered for safety).

## Redistributing Rooms

If you have more than one child, space is limited, and you really put your children's well-being and comfort before your own, it *could* be more practical to give up the master bedroom, at least until the teenage years, and turn it into a really good-sized bedroom-playroom with as much built-in storage as possible. Consider the advantages. Such rooms often get the best light during the day, which is far better used for play purposes than wasted, as it so often is since few of us see much of the interior of our bedrooms during the day. (That way, too, you might then be able to keep the living room and kitchen tidier and comparatively toy-free.) If you put two or more children in the big room together, you can also use the smaller rooms that they would have had for extra dressing room-clothes storage space, or as study adjuncts, or both, to your now much smaller bedroom, which will then become more of a suite. It's not such a bad deal.

WHEN DECORATING A CHILD'S ROOM, KEEP IN MIND THAT CHILDREN'S TASTES CHANGE FAST WITH THE YEARS.

*Accent a muted primary color with a matching middle tone for a lovely and lively color scheme. With pretty fabrics and accessories, it's easy to adapt the room décor for the appropriate age.*

Once children reach the age where they can draw and paint, play with models, and write, they will need an adjustable desk or table lamp, and a lamp or adjustable wall light by the bed. However, these may not be necessary yet if there are already recessed down-lights or ceiling lights over the bed and play/work stations with the requisite two-way switches. As children get older, they will, of course, need more lamps.

## WINDOWS

Once you have established that windows are quite safe and will withstand the best efforts of enquiring and adventurous children to climb out of them, the best way of dealing with them is either to shutter them with louvered shutters or with various kinds of louvered or fabric shades rather than curtains, which can tugged at and sometimes pulled down altogether by toddlers. Louvers are always good because they can be adjusted to either filter or block out the light altogether. If fabric

Roman or roller shades are preferred, and you want to keep out the morning light as long as possible, attach them to hang outside the window frames rather than within the reveals, and make sure that they have blackout linings.

## COLORS

There is no doubt that white walls painted in a washable paint are practical as a background for dual-purpose sleep/play rooms. When the wiping or washing off of marks and scribbles becomes inadequate for the task, the area can easily be repainted without too much worry about matching old colors (however, since whites vary too, remember the *kind* of white you used if you plan to repaint one worn area as opposed to the whole room). The white can always be cheered up with a colorful trim for baseboards, door, and even window surrounds, or with borders, especially the self-adhesive kind that can be stuck on and peeled off and changed on a whim. Also, white makes a good, useful background for all the other colorful things that inevitably collect in a growing child's room: toys, toy boxes, books, posters, painted furniture, fabrics, and so on.

Of course, in a rearguard action against dirt and dirty marks, you could always paint the room a darker, warmer color, a navy or grass green, or even a rosy red, especially if the room gets very little natural daylight, and then brighten it with a gleaming white trim. Washable vinyl wallpaper can be kept pretty clean-looking, but when choosing it, keep it as simple, or two-toned or tone-on-tone, as possible, again to act as a good background for all the other accumulated colors. There are numerous themed pictorial children's wallpapers to choose from now, along with themed accessories. However, it is generally a mistake to spend too much money on themed wallpapers, or trying to achieve a particular theme; today's most pressing desire will probably be deemed completely un-cool in a year's time.

*Pets often cozy up in children's beds for daytime and nighttime napping. If this is the case in your home, brush your cat daily to remove loose hairs before they overtake your blankets, carpets, and upholstery.*

*Bedding and accessories in solid shades accented with changeable patterns and prints allow a boy's room to grow along with the child. A table for models and puzzles is a nice addition, as is a desk for doing homework.*

Whether you use paint or wallpaper for the walls, try to always use Blue-Tak rather than paste or sticky tape, because this rarely leaves any sort of mark in its wake.

Upholstery and any fabric window treatments, on the other hand, can take as much pattern as you like, since the denser the pattern, the less show of wear and tear. But again, its wise to keep pattern to fairly classic or timeless designs such as checks or two-toned *toiles de Jouey*, which will both stand the test of rapidly changing tastes and look good with the rapid onslaught of new colors in accessories.

## FLOORING

The main requirements for children's flooring is that it is as sound-absorbent as it is easy to clean and maintain and that it is soft enough to cushion frequent falls. If you decide on carpet, which is certainly the most sound-resistant type of flooring, it would be wise, if you have the choice, to pick a variety made from one of the synthetic fibers that is particularly stain resistant. Avoid high piles because they are a deterrent to wheeled toys as well as dirt collects. Cork and vinyl, and cushioned vinyl, are easy to clean, reasonably sound-proof, and reasonably soft; plus, they look good with rugs, which also helps the sound-absorbency. Wood, though always handsome, is not such a good idea in a child's room, because it can splinter, is not particularly sound-proof, and can stain unless very well-varnished.

## FURNITURE

Apart from the crib, it is perfectly possible to find furniture that will keep pace with a child's changing needs. Depending on the size of the room or the length of the designated wall, a series of two or three or even four unpainted or unfinished chests of drawers, with one or two kneehole spaces left in between, can be topped with an easily cleanable length of white laminate or lacquered butcher block, and can then serve first as a changing surface (with a changing tray) and general dumping space, then as a play surface, and finally as a work surface with space for a computer and, if the top is long enough, a television and stereo as well. Later still, one section could be used as a dressing table with a mirror. The color of the painted finish you use can, of course, be changed whenever needed. Of course, the size of the chair or chairs may have to change, though you could buy an adjustable-height swivel chair normally used for hairdressers from a commercial outfitters.

If you use a cart with a changing tray for the infant stage, with a second level for diapers, creams, and so on, it can well go on as a base for a TV or a movable occasional table—again with a change of color if necessary. If there is more than one child, or your child likes to have an extra bed for a friend's sleepover, you might entertain the idea of buying the stacking variety, which can be dismantled later to form two sofa beds. With many of these models you can buy drawers to fit underneath for extra storage.

## Comfort Zoning
### SOUND ABSORPTION BASICS

Children's rooms should contain as many soft, sound-absorbing surfaces as possible (for everyone else's comfort). Rugs on top of carpeting, fabric on walls, and those long, stuffed rolls of fabric used as draft-dodgers at the bottom of doors can all be used to deaden the sound of too-loud music.

WHEN THE CHILDREN BECOME TEENAGERS, ENCOURAGE THEM TO HAVE AS MANY RUGS AS POSSIBLE PILED ON TOP OF THE CARPET. THE MORE SOUND-DEADENERS, THE BETTER.

OPPOSITE: *Years ago, a canopy bed was something special to transform a young girl's room into a fantasy chamber. Today, the elegance and sophistication of a canopy bed can appeal to young and old alike. The beds can be designed in various ways to suit different tastes and decorating schemes.*

*In a child's world of make-believe, anything can happen. Be sure to provide lots of play-time opportunities for your children to explore and enjoy their thoughts and imagination.*

AS CHILDREN TURN INTO ADOLESCENTS, THEY SHOULD BE ALLOWED TO CHOOSE WHAT THEIR OWN ROOMS LOOK LIKE, AS FAR AS IT IS PRACTICABLE AND AFFORDABLE. AT THE VERY LEAST THEY SHOULD BE OFFERED A NUMBER OF PRE-BUDGETED CHOICES SO THAT THEY FEEL THE FINAL DECISION HAS BEEN THEIR OWN. LET THEM USE THEIR IMAGINATION AND TRY OUT THEIR OWN TASTES AS MUCH AS YOU CAN. IT'S THE ONLY WAY FOR THEM TO LEARN.

Alternatively, you can ensure that a child's first twin bed is of the trundle variety with a second bed for friends (or another child) that can be pulled out from underneath. The original nursing chair, if you nursed in the child's room, can well stay in the room, with the odd re-covering, for years. And small, sturdy occasional tables can go on being used forever.

## STORAGE

Trying to keep a kid's room tidy is like trying to dig a hole in wet sand or hold back the tide or almost any other impossible act. Since out of sight is generally out of mind, as much built-in storage as possible is as much a necessity for most children from toddlers to teenagers as it is for ardent advocates of minimilism. However, this is not always possible for reasons of space or finance.

Happily, there are enough inventive, cheerful, and comparatively inexpensive alternatives around to make practical substitutes. And the more fun they look, the more they are likely to be used. If money is in really short supply for amusing temporary storage, there are various things you can do yourself. These are tried and tested ideas:

- Look out for old gym lockers in junk yards, garage sales, and second-hand stores, or buy them from institutional suppliers. Paint them in different shades of bright glossy paint (one shade for each child if you have several). They can be adapted for hanging clothes or, fitted with shelves, will hold toys, big flat books, and games as well. Fitting them with shelves will also obviate any risk of the child climbing in and getting trapped. In any event, try to get the locking process neutralized.
- For older children, find old or inexpensive unfinished wood cupboards, paint them, and use them as a storage base and platform for a mattress placed on top and reached by a small painted or lacquered ladder. Depending upon the age of the child, you can add removable safety rails.
- Use a window or door wall to make an entire row of shelf and cupboard storage. Fit 2-inch-by-4-inch (5-cm-by-10-cm) around the window or door and turn them into shelves of different heights. Add extra support with a row of edge-to-edge low lockers, painted unfinished wood chests, or old trunks. The tops of these latter will provide a good play surface. The narrower shelves will hold books and boxed games, and the lockers or chests can hold almost anything.
- If your handyman skills are slight, don't bother with the shelves. Just put a series of wooden boxes with lift-up lids down one wall, paint them all one color or different colors, and cover the tops with slabs of thick foam enclosed by washable, removable cotton slipcovers to make seating as well as storage units. Add brightly colored scatter pillows for extra comfort.
- Just use large, brightly colored baskets or hampers for different toys, or string up canvas bags and pouches for soft storage.

- Those striped cotton or canvas old bathing tent-like storage units looks like fun and are decorative and comparatively cheap to buy.
- You can almost always find reasonably priced, large wooden chests or trunks or bright new ones. Put them at the end of the beds to hold toys, sweaters, sports equipment, and so on, as well as to provide extra seats.

## A FINAL THOUGHT

Once children are old enough to make choices, it will help their independence of mind and their confidence in their own taste to let them choose their own color schemes, at least as far as it is practicable and affordable. However, until they have proved a certain sensibility, it might be more practical to give them some parameters within the choice, for example, "you can do any of these but not those." Or give them the chance to choose from among several schemes. Once they have proved themselves, as it were, they should be allowed to generally add their own character to their rooms by painting murals, hanging fabric, and putting up their own posters and chosen art.

*Playing and studying are essential parts of childhood. Be sure to have space in your child's room for both activities, with adequate light for reading and lots of shelves to store books and toys.*

# BATHROOMS AND POWDER ROOMS
## Calm Oases

*Ideas about comfort in the bathroom veer as wildly as definitions about comfort itself, depending as much upon tastes as on circumstances.*

There is no doubt that a bathroom to oneself, be it just a shower room, is as important to the general comfort and well-being of many people as Virginia Woolf's proverbial "A Room of One's Own." Whatever your ideal bathroom is, though, basically the choices boil down to three questions: How much money can be set aside for the project? How much space is there? Do you want a really luxurious room or a spare, thoroughly practical, minimalist splashing place?

We are so used to comfortably designed and, indeed, comforting bathrooms that we take them for granted, except when we agonize about how new ones should be designed or old ones revamped. Yet it took well over a thousand years for Westerners to even begin to emulate some of the everyday comforts taken for granted in the ancient world.

Fourth-century Romans used six times as much water per head as Londoners in the late 1980s. And remember: The population was really very small at that time. According to *Clean and Decent,* Lawrence Wright's invaluable history of the bath (Routledge & Paul, 1960), Rome in the fourth century had eleven public baths,

ABOVE: *Bathroom niceties, like dried flowers and potpourri, scented soaps, and embroidered hand towels, turn this functional room into a perfumed oasis.*

LEFT: *Antique colored and cut glass bottles add vintage charm to a washroom. Freshen with flowers and plants in pretty vases.*

OPPOSITE: *A comfortable bathroom is a place where you can escape from life's worries and find a moment of peace. This bathroom has a cabinet for storing toiletries and chair that doubles as a side table or shelf.*

ABOVE: *There is an endless variety of styles, colors, sizes, and shapes of bathroom sinks. This sink blends with the architectural elements as well as the vintage of the house.*

1,352 fountains and cisterns, and 856 private baths. Some private houses in Pompeii are believed to have had as many as thirty faucets, as well as private flushing toilets. And there were plenty of public ones too. On the other hand, the Anglo-Saxons hardly had a specific *bath*room to call their own until well into the seventeenth century. At Canterbury in Kent, England, for example, a complete water service was installed in the monastery in 1150, and since it was one of the few communities to have escaped death during the Black Plague of 1349, one imagines that the system may still have been in reasonable repair two hundred years later. It is also a fact that medieval books of etiquette insisted upon the washing of hands, face, and teeth every morning, and the washing of hands before and after meals (only practical, one supposes, given that people ate with their fingers); but they made no particular mention of bathing, though baths certainly existed and were mostly built to allow several people to bathe at once. Since there were no pipes, hot water was scarce, so whole families and their guests would bathe and carouse together, which was presumably more sociable than sanitary. There was apparently no inhibition about men and women bathing together. By the nineteenth century running water became quite widespread, although it

was still rarely piped above the basement and servants had to run up and down stairs with jugs of steaming water. Portable baths came in all shapes and sizes.

By the end of the nineteenth century, almost every respectable house in the United States and Europe had at least one bathroom converted from a former bedroom, and new town houses were being built with integral bathrooms containing handsome toilets sculpted and decorated with floral motifs, acanthus leaves, Greek key designs, and goodness knows what else. Bathtubs, by now plumbed in, were often elaborated outside with veined marble or at least simulated marble. On the other hand, in rural areas farmhouses and cottages still had outhouses or privies in the yard with commodes and chamber pots still part of bedroom accoutrements. And this state of affairs often continued until late in the twentieth century, even though the entire concept of bathroom comfort and design began to change in the 1920s. This was not only the time when American hotels started providing a bathroom for every bedroom, but the period of an important technological discovery that involved color-matching items made from different materials. In short, the glassy china used to make toilet bowls and sinks could now be matched to the enameled cast iron of bathtubs. Eureka! The colored bathroom suite, which became for a time quite a status symbol.

ABOVE: *This bathroom with its marble vanity sink and sunken marble tub is the picture of elegance. The geometric designs along the base coordinate beautifully with the striped wallpaper and classically inspired wall art.*

OPPOSITE BOTTOM: *Bathroom fixtures can underscore the style of the room as well as serve as a backdrop to other decorative features. White is a favorite bathroom color, as it can go with every décor, from modern to traditional.*

# Creating a Serene Bathroom

*Washbasins need enough space in front and on the sides of them to allow one to wash with ease. The sink countertop should have enough room to fit a glass, a bar of soap, and the similar.*

Although most bathrooms look deceptively simple, they are almost as hard as kitchens to plan; and since so many are rather small, they need to be planned down to the last inch. It is ironic that so many different specialists are needed to work on a room that will generally sustain only very few permutations of arrangement. Think about it. The average small bathroom has a bathtub, a shower (in or out of the bath), a sink, a john, a mirror, some sort of lighting, some sort of cabinet or storage unit, and maybe a bidet. It will have tiles or marble or both, or maybe granite. There will of course be a floor, and possibly a window.

This may seem to be an extraordinary list. But to put all of this together there usually is a general contractor, a plumber, an electrician, probably a carpenter, a tile and/or marble installer, possibly a different floor person, someone to install the mirrors, someone to paint and maybe to hang wallpaper, and someone to put up whatever you have decided for the window. That's a lot of people for one comparatively small space.

## FIXTURES

Every inch counts in so many bathrooms, which is why it is useful to know as much as you can about the average measurements of standard equipment. Being aware of the optimum amount of clearance to allow around each fixture, as well as the minimum headroom to allow, will ensure much more comfort for the room as well as for the user.

- The average bathtub is 60 inches (152.4 cm) long and needs 86 inches (218.4 cm) in headroom.
- A bathroom floor will need a massive amount of reinforcement in order to support a bathtub big enough to take two *comfortably*.
- A toilet needs 24 inches (61 cm) of clearance space in front of it. Make sure that there is enough space between the rim of the seat and the wall in front of it to allow plenty of room for knees.
- A bidet also needs 24 inches (61 cm) of uncluttered space in front of it with at least 8 inches (20.3 cm) of space to the sides and back to make room for the legs. A bidet will also need a minimum ceiling height of 78 inches (198 cm).
- A washbasin needs to be sited with enough space in front of it—an optimum of 28 inches (71 cm)—to allow you to comfortably bend over to wash, and plenty of elbow room at each side—about 8 inches (20.3 cm). It is not comfortable to wash at a basin jammed up against the side of a wall.
- The sink countertop should have a generous space for glasses, soaps, creams, make-up, etc., or at the very least, a capacious glass shelf.

- There is no standard height to set a wash basin. If you are small you will need it set lower; if you are tall it will need to be higher. But remember, it is hugely uncomfortable to the back for tall people to have to crouch low over a basin to wash their face. And not easy for small people to have to stand on tiptoe to do the same. Mismatched partners, at least heightwise, should consider different-height basins in different parts of the bathroom, if it is big enough. Twin basins sunk into or perched on a counter are not for them. The ideal, of course, is separate bathrooms. A separate shower needs at least 36 inches (91 cm) of clearance on the sides away from the wall.

- Older people, or people with bad backs, will find it difficult to clamber in and out of a bathtub and so will definitely need a free-standing shower. Make sure there are plenty of handles fixed in useful places to grip and that older people have a nonslip seat to sit on under the shower, with safe controls at the right level.

*Most bathroom windows are best with louvered or fabric shades or shutters. Combine shades with an attractive swag to soften the lines of the window and to add color to the room.*

RIGHT: *Try to have as much storage room as possible in the bath for towels and wash-cloths, bath toys, and other items. Keep cleaning supplies out of sight and out of the reach of small children.*

OPPOSITE: *Sometimes a shower stall is too awkward to accom-modate a glass door or screen. In that case, hang a curtain or even a pair of curtains that can be drawn to either side when the shower is not in use.*

*A small cabinet storing hand towels and facecloths can be conveniently set by a basin or tub.*

## ORGANIZATION

With the best will in the world it is almost impossible to keep a family bathroom looking either elegant or tidy, let alone comfortable. All too often towels are dropped in soggy heaps, bath toys are left abandoned in bathtubs, shelves are filled with old toothbrushes, and the edges of bathtubs are lined with an unsightly array of half-used bottles. What can be done? Plenty.

### STORAGE

Fit in as much storage as possible. See that there are cupboards or cabinets where bath toys can be stashed away, preferably in one basket; where cleaning things can be concealed but are within easy reach of everybody; and, if possible, where everyone can be given a separate shelf for his or her own toiletry. In fact, if there is space, a whole row of mirrored cabinets along one wall would look quite hand-some. Or even a row of kitchen cabinets. Also put up rows of hooks in as many places as you can: on the back of the door for dressing gowns; by the bathtub for facecloths; by the wash basin(s) for hand towels.

### ORGANIZING TOWELS AND FACECLOTHS

Have separate, different-colored towels and facecloths for each member of the family and *stick* to those colors. One advantage of everyone having his or her own particular-colored towels is that you will know in a flash whose towels have ended up on the floor. An added bonus is that if you have an all-white tiled bath-room, the different colored towels will look good.

# Shower Curtains

Glass doors on a shower stall, or a glass screen added to a shower above a bathtub, is a great deal more efficacious in keeping the rest of the bathroom dry than a shower curtain; they are easier to keep clean and neat, will avoid splashes better, and will not attract mold as much as shower curtains. Nevertheless, it is not always possible to install doors or a screen because of the expense, or the awkwardness of the space, or even, occasionally, for aesthetic preference, in which case there is no alternative but to hang a the shower curtain.

If you do install curtains there are several ways to make them work as well as possible.

■ Make sure that the inset ceiling track or pole on which a shower curtain is hung is longer than the projection of the shower spray. It is usually safer to have two curtains that can then be drawn or looped back to either side when the shower is not in use. If they are made of the fabric of your choice facing towards the room with a separate waterproof plastic lining behind them, they will look much better and will go on looking good for longer, since the inner plastic lining can be replaced if it starts getting moldy or stiff and crackling.

■ The actual plastic or treated voile shower curtains will last longer if they are always dried after use. This, however, is generally a council of perfection, especially in a family bathroom. In any event, they should at least be given a good clean and dry once a week. (In fact, every effort should be made in a family bathroom to afford a glass screen. The money will be well spent.)

■ If the shower is over a bathtub, make sure that the shower curtains are drawn in place *inside* the tub. It sounds like elementary advice, but it is advice that often goes unheeded, with a resulting deluge spilling onto the bathroom floor.

## Comfort Zoning

**ELECTRICAL SAFETY BASICS**

It is absolutely essential that you do not use any electrical appliances such as irons or radiant electric heaters anywhere near water. Radiant electrical heaters should be fixed as high as possible and controlled with a switch.

*To help towels dry more quickly, either install heated towel rails or place a rod for towels over a long radiator.*

You should also fit in as many heated towel rails as you can and insist that everyone picks up his or her own towels and places them neatly on the racks. Or have a long radiator going the length of one wall with a rod for towels above it. This way towels will at least dry quickly. Finally, make sure that everyone has a roomy clothes hamper in his or her bedroom so that there is no reason to leave discarded clothes around the bathroom.

## TEMPERATURE CONTROL

One of the most important ingredients for comfort in a bathroom is getting the room the right temperature: evenly warm in the winter and cool enough in summer or hot climates.

If you can possibly install a heated towel rail or two you should do so, but beware of the kind that is run solely off the central heating system. This is fine when the heating is operational, but what about when it is not? To make sure of warm, dry towels at all times, try to buy electric towel racks that have thermostats or that run off the hot-water system.

If a hot-water heater is placed in a cupboard in the bathroom, this will help keep the room warm in winter (although it can make the room uncomfortably hot in summer). If you do not have the room or the budget for a radiator of some sort, extra warmth—and coolness—can be provided by a wall-mounted fan heater; extra warmth alone can be generated by an infrared heater mounted above the door or a mirror.

## LIGHTING

The bathroom, as do most rooms, requires both general or ambient light as well as specific light, for shaving and make-up. However, if a room is really small with a lower than average ceiling in which it is impossible to recess ceiling light, or to use a ceiling fixture, you should at least ensure that the mirror lights are bright enough to supply general light as well.

Wall lights on either side of the bathroom mirror or Hollywood strips all around the edge of a mirror (preferably attached to a dimmer switch) are best for make-up and shaving, or just above if only for shaving. You can also buy mirrors with strips of light all around, or inset with light strips.

If a room is large enough to be more of a bathroom-dressing room, it can be made to look particularly comfortable with strip light concealed behind curtains, valances, or a valance over a shade. If you have a reasonable ceiling recess, you can also install eyeball spots in the ceiling and attach them to a dimmer switch to illuminate any art or plants or objects. Small internal bathrooms, or any small bathroom come to that, could have an illuminated ceiling panel, or lights concealed behind a "floating" panel or false ceiling. Separate showers can be lit by a waterproof down-light recessed into the ceiling if possible, otherwise ceiling mounted.

## WINDOWS

Unless a bathroom has been formed from a large converted bedroom and has correspondingly gracious windows that are far enough from water sources to be curtained, most bathroom windows are best with louvered shades of some sort, or fabric shades or shutters. A nice alternative is to build shelves across a window that is not looked into and use it to display a collection of colored glass or plants. Most plants thrive in steam, and whether or not you install shelves across windows, you can still put one or two or more plants on a windowsill. Another alternative is to have a stained-glass panel, or inset stained-glass panels—an ingredient found in many nineteenth-century town houses.

## COLORS

Apart from the natural colors of marble or granite, mosaic or wood, most bathrooms look best either white with relieving colors in trim, towels, and accessories or in a color that flatters the skin. Cheerful and warm as a yellow might be, the light reflected from it does not help a face in the early morning. Similarly, however cool a pale pistachio green, it can only add a certain sickliness. Subtle paint colors such as a deep ecru or putty or camel with a white trim, and white or red or black towels, look comfortably handsome.

*In bathrooms, you can use practical items as accessories. Towels can be displayed in baskets or on rails, and colorful bottles of shampoo, perfume, lotion, and the like can be decoratively arranged on countertops.*

## WALLS

Family bathrooms, even bathrooms just shared by a couple, are generally more practical if they are tiled, either with ceramic tiles, quarry tiles, earthenware tiles, marble, mosaic, mirrored mosaic, glass tiles, bricks, or granite. Tiles withstand steam and splashes, are easier to clean, and always look neat. Exotically patterned Spanish, Italian, and Mexican ceramic or earthenware tiles look at the very least intriguing. .Marble and granite look definitely sumptuous. Any kind of plain tile can be made to look particularly elegant with contrasting borders used to give the look of panels, or to outline mirrors, doors, and windows. Moreover, some people *feel* more comfortable by the very fact that tiles *look* practical. Other people, however, find tiles rather hard-edged and cold-looking, even though they can be considerably softened by large, fluffy towels, fabric window treatments, and even a (preferably nylon) carpet. Some prefer warmer-looking alternatives—for instance, tongue-and-groove boarding that has been sealed and varnished or given several coats of lacquer, or at least a coat of semi-gloss paint, or just semi-gloss paint with some 18 inches (45 cm) of tiles around the basin and bathtub and inside any separate shower.

Although it is usually a disaster to use wallpaper or any sort of wall covering (apart from wood) in a family bathroom because it starts to peel and look unkempt in no time, there is really no reason why personal bathrooms—that is to say, bathrooms not only used by just one person, but rooms that are particularly personal and idiosyncratic to look at—can sport what they like on the walls. Wallpaper (especially wallpaper given a couple of coats of semi-gloss or eggshell polyurethane for extra wear); lacquer or another decorative paint finish; garden trellis; paneling; even fabric such as burlap or cotton or wool—above a protective wainscot or dado of tiles, marble, or tongue-and-groove wood—will all make a bathroom look warm and comfortable, or cool and comfortable, as required.

Painted and papered and tongue-and-grooved walls can all take a collection of prints or photographs or various collections, even a collection of mirrors. It is even possible to hang art on a tiled surface by fixing hooks into the grouting.

## FLOORING

The most important point to bear in mind about any bathroom floor is that it must be slip-proof. However handsome they are, ceramic or natural stone tiles that are not slip- or skid-proof can be quite lethal as soon as they get wet. Rot- and damp-resistant carpet such as the various nylon and Terylene varieties are certainly comfortable underfoot and provide a nice contrast to a tiled surface. Well-sealed wood always looks good, especially with cotton tumbletwist rugs or, in a nonfamily bathroom, oriental, nomadic, kelims or ethnic rugs. Cork and vinyl are practical in a family or children's bathroom, as are vinyl tiles.

## Comfort Zoning
### CONDENSATION BASICS

Condensation can be quite a nuisance in bathrooms. However, steamed-up mirrors and windows can largely be avoided, or at least lessened, by steady warmth and by adequate ventilation. If you do not want to open a window in the winter, install an extractor fan on the outside wall or in the window itself. It, and the sort of extractor fan that is obligatory in all internal bathrooms, will keep the bathroom from fogging up. Mirrors with built-in lights that warm the glass will also help to eliminate condensation.

ABOVE: *Live plants thrive in bathrooms that have some light and are a good decorating choice in most bathrooms.*

OPPOSITE: *Combine tiles in contrasting colors for a practical yet polished look. Soften the scheme with big, fluffy towels and fabric curtains and upholstery.*

# Guest Bathrooms

## DECORATING A POWDER ROOM

If bathrooms are one of the hardest rooms in the house to design well, then powder rooms are some of the most fun to decorate. Because they are generally very small you can be as fanciful and extravagant as you like, using fabrics, wallpapers, and so on that you would think extravagant to use in a larger space.

Putting a handsome fabric on the walls is one option. Massing the bathroom with memorabilia is another. Install beautiful lights and a lot of mirror and, depending on the location and climate, have fun with that little bit of floor. Of course, what could be better in a hot climate than to come into a cool limestone- or granite-lined room with brushed steel fittings. Or on a cold day to wash up in a beautifully paneled and lit denlike room, or one with some mahogany bookshelves full of books that you'd actually like to stay and browse through.

*Use scented candles and potpourri to make your powder room more pleasant. Place dried flowers in pretty vases or tie dried eucalyptus leaves up with ribbon for an attractive and fragrant display.*

## STOCKING A GUEST BATHROOM

Like guest bedrooms, it is ideal if guest bathrooms can show regard for a guest's comforts. The best towels you can buy, warmed on a heated towel rack, is always a thoughtful gesture; so are spare new toothbrushes, toothpaste, razors, analgesics, bandages and plasters for minor cuts, mouthwash, clean hairbrushes and combs, a clothes brush, a hair blower, and soap for hand-washing undergarments, in case any of these items have been forgotten.

Other items you will want to put out are good facial and bath soap, along with bath essences and oils, shampoo and conditioner, talcum powder, toilet water (both men's and women's), cleansing cream, moisturizer, facial tissues, and cotton balls.

*Make guest bathrooms more welcoming with piles of soft towels, an assortment of good soaps, and a generous supply of cleansers and lotions.*

# TERRACES, DECKS, AND PORCHES

## The Joy of Open Spaces

*Beguiling outdoor living areas are a much-coveted adjunct
to a home, especially in the summer months in so-called
temperate climates, And, of course, all year round in hot
areas where indoor-outdoor living is a large part of daily life.
All the more reason, then, to make any such outdoor spaces
as comfortable, and as easily workable, as you can,
whatever their size, type, and location.*

Decks, verandahs, terraces, loggias, and so on are, of course, basically outdoor rooms, outside adjuncts to the living space. At their best, they are shaded by trees and plants; scented by flowers; and lulled by the sound and sight of the sea or a lake or the river, or the splash and shimmer of a pool, or a stunning view of mountains, or even just a garden. Or, in the case of an urban front porch, by the familiar street outside. And because they are such fortunate adjuncts to the home, wherever that home is situated, they should be designed and furnished for the maximum enjoyment of those hopefully languid days and velvety nights—with the most appropriate furniture, accessories, table settings, barbecues, pools, hot tubs, and, most particularly, lighting—for safety, as much as for its decorative effect.

ABOVE: *Porches, terraces, decks, and even backyard dining areas should be designed and furnished for maximum comfort and enjoyment. Set chairs to overlook scenic views for moments of quiet contemplation.*

LEFT AND OPPOSITE: *When entertaining, set the table with fresh fruits and flowers to add to the pleasure of the gardens.*

# Creating a Calming Outdoor Space

ON A WINDLESS EVENING, NOTHING IS MORE CHARMING AND CALMING THAN THE GENTLE FLICKERING OF A MASS OF DIFFERENTLY SHAPED CANDLES IN DIFFERENT CONTAINERS.

## LIGHTING

Since there are few things more rewarding than coming home from a hot, busy workday (or a hot, action-packed holiday) with the anticipation of relaxing on that porch or terrace or verandah, one of the first things one must get right is the lighting. Drinking and eating dinner outside means that night will have descended long before the evening is finished. As always, the sort of lighting you decide upon will absolutely depend on location and style.

Candlelight is always an immediate answer to summer outdoor lighting. And if the candles are mainly citronella, you will also be preventing the irritating dislocation of all that delicious night air by an onslaught of mosquitoes.

Try putting night-lights in small colored glasses in front of each plate. Light tall candelabra to vary the pace; amass a collection of storm lanterns; group a collection of small fruit or vegetable candles or different height candlesticks in the center of the table. Put candles on side tables too. They will look magical. But make sure to keep flames away from leaves and shrubbery. And be careful that candles do not tumble out of holders.

### SUBTLETY IN LIGHTING

Despite the presence of candlelight, you often need some sort of subtle background or ambient light for serving food, collecting plates, sorting wines and pouring accurately, and so on. However, a little light goes a very long way in the dark. Wall-hung lanterns are good, combined with some gentle up-lighting among the leaves. Up-lights can also be used to great advantage to gently focus light on an urn or hanging basket, some architectural feature, a statue, or a fountain, or even just to bounce light off the inside of a porch or verandah roof.

*One of the first things to take care of when planning an outdoor dinner party is the lighting. Candlelight is always lovely, especially if there are citronella candles to keep mosquitoes at bay.*

If you look out over a garden, or a natural-looking backyard, or onto trees, this is a good opportunity to show off those features. Lawns, hedges, tree trunks, the patterns of leaves, stone or brick paths, and old walls all look magnified and infinitely more restful in night light. And an imaginatively lit path or sweep of grass will look gratifying with what amounts nowadays to stage effects, so good and varied is modern outdoor lighting. Just angling outdoor spots up through leaves and onto the rough texture of bark, or swooshing an arc of light along a herbaceous border or formal pots of boxwood, will add enormously to the pleasure of the outdoors.

Although it is interesting and fun to experiment indoors with work lights, I would advise seeking some professional lighting help for the exterior, simply because a little light does indeed go a long way—and because it is difficult.

*Lanterns can be set in the center of a dining table and on side tables and ledges for a subtle ambience. If there are trees, shrubs, and potted plants about, the light will create a pretty patterning through the branches and leaves.*

### LIGHTING FOR SAFETY

However, lighting up the porch, terrace, verandah, garden, yard, and front entrance to a house, for that matter, is not *just* for ornamentation. It is also for identification, safety, and security, which are, of course, comforting things in themselves. One of the main things to remember is that at night what is *not* lit, is to all intents and purposes invisible. Another is that light that is not very well thought-out can cause disturbing and often disorientating contrasts of brightness and darkness. Luckily,

*The outdoor space should visually relate to the indoor space. When decorating an adjacent patio, consider how the exterior arrangement and lighting will appear from the inside and vice versa.*

## Comfort Zoning

### OUTDOOR LIGHTING BASICS

Outdoor lighting equipment, of course, is somewhat different from the indoor variety because it has to meet certain criteria. It has to be moisture-proof and occasionally submersible (as for pool lighting) and certainly weather tight so that rain, snow, mud, dust, or extremes of temperature will not affect it. It should be built of non-corroding material and should only be connected through a ground fault interrupter that can turn off the electricity, in case of defective equipment or an accidental grounding, before anyone can get a shock. This sort of safety problem can best be avoided by using low-voltage equipment, particularly in a small garden or on a terrace, or when lighting climbers or low shrubs on the façade of an average-size house, and especially when there are small children. Solar lights are a great idea for lighting paths and so on, but they are not so amenable to fingertip control as far as decorative lighting is concerned. In any event, it is advisable to get an electrician to install outdoor lighting equipment for safety's sake as well as for his or her judgment of exactly how much light will be needed for what.

after the initial shock of contrast, eyes adapt fairly quickly to the dark so that quite low levels of illumination are sufficient to see by. However, whatever the level, careful shielding of some sort should always be used to prevent glare. And, as in indoor lighting during the day, outdoor lighting is much subtler if light sources are hidden and the light is reflected *from* walls, trees, or shrubs.

On the identification, safety, and security front, it is only common sense to think about front-of-house lighting. Lighted house numbers, visible from the street, are thoughtful courtesies for guests, who might be unfamiliar with the exact whereabouts of your home. Doorways, porches, and keyholes should be lit to make it easy for householders to let themselves in and out, and to make it equally easy to identify callers, as well as to deter prowlers. Make sure too that any steps are well-lit with attention to both treads and risers. Walkways and paths should be easy to see along, and any possible obstacles should be well-illuminated.

If there is any sort of garden or yard spreading away from the house, you can light up the perimeters to create a feeling of enclosure. To emphasize the relationship between the house and the grounds it is set in, there should be some lit feature, or features, right outside the house, such as a path or a group of shrubs.

### THE INDOOR-OUTDOOR RELATIONSHIP

It is also a good idea to make sure that the *inside* of a house should somehow be visually related to the outside. On a fine night, a large window with no curtains, shades, or shutters, or with the window coverings drawn back, can seem like an uncomfortable and quite disconcerting dark hole unless you have some sort of exterior vista (quite apart from the mirror effect that is often created on the window glass, with the reflection of the interior jumbling up with any objects immediately outside, such as garden chairs or flowerpots). In this case, always use a dimmer switch to lower the light in the room and balance it with exterior light to the point where distracting reflections on the glass will vanish.

If you light the floor of a porch, patio, terrace, loggia, verandah, deck, yard, or garden that is just outside a living area, you at least provide some sort of continuity with the inside floor. But you could also light a vertical surface: a wall, a line of shrubs, a hedge. And, as I have touched on already, it would be a waste not to take advantage of the sort of effects that can be achieved with artificial light that are simply not possible in daylight: up-light shining into trees, light grazing an urn and revealing its detail, the silhouette of a finely shaped shrub or decorative tree in a pot, the glow of ornamental water or a swimming pool. And when you are outside, do not underestimate the attraction of any light seen coming from the inside, whether it is glowing through curtains or shades or giving glimpses of interiors.

## FLOORING

The floors of decks and porches, of course, are almost always tongue-and-groove wood, as are most verandahs, but terraces, patios, and loggias that are right off living areas are usually paved in some way, either with flagstones, paving stones, or nonslip tiles. However, if the living area has a limestone, travertine, slate, or tiled floor, for example, there is no reason why that same nonslip material cannot be run onto the outdoor area as well. This will make the area seem much larger as well as producing a pleasing sense of continuity.

*Outdoor light should be subtle yet strong enough to properly reveal passageways, doors, and stairs. This row of hanging lanterns has a whimsical feel, yet it will illuminate the path for nighttime visitors.*

*Deck and porch floors are usually made of wood, as seen here, while terraces, patios, and loggias are usually paved either with stone or tile.*

## PRIVACY

However glamorous you manage to make your outdoor spaces, you will also want to spend equal attention on making the area as private as possible. Dense hedges are one solution, and the denser the better for sound absorption as well. If there is already a garden wall and you are surrounded by neighbors, you might need to make the divisions somewhat higher. Unless your neighbors agree with you about raising the height of the actual walls, the easiest and most aesthetically pleasing solution is to add lattice screens, up which you can grow vigorous and preferably sweet-smelling climbing plants and roses. Of course, if the space is large enough, you can plant trees and large shrubs; but these require time to grow enough to provide the necessary screening.

## FOUNTAINS AND POOLS

Some sort of water feature is an attractive addition to most terraces, patios, and loggias, though not necessarily so practical on a porch, deck, or verandah unless it happens to be a practical outdoor shower on a beach house deck, or a hot tub, or one of the kit-types—plastic-lined, half-barrel-shaped plug-in pools.

Fountains can be as charming to the ears as the eyes, as can, if the space is large enough, a small ornamental pond on a terrace, and, naturally, if the backyard or garden is large enough, a swimming or plunge pool. Even if the latter are not immediately affordable, there are still much cheaper pools that can be installed aboveground, and perhaps landscaped in somehow.

## FURNITURE

Any outdoor furniture you buy should be able to withstand any sort of unkind weather as well as a lot of sun. Unless you have a great deal of storage space and some strong, healthy, willing friends or family members to lug heavy pieces back and forth, you are much better off buying sturdy pieces that can remain permanently in place. If you are buying extra-heavy pieces, it is a bonus if they come with wheels in case you want to move the pieces in and out of the sun. Long chaises for sunbathers, for example, will be much more maneuverable and can take maximum advantage of those moving rays.

Of course what you buy, and in what materials and shapes, depends as usual upon suitability and budget. A nice, old, battered refectory table will look splendid on a farmhouse porch or under a leafy arbor, but not so good on a contemporary, sophisticated–looking terrace. Weathered slatted wood pieces look great on a sun-baked deck, not so good under a gracefully pillared verandah. Old porches tend to look best with a mishmash of old things: battered couches, a hammock or old glider, some rocking chairs, a cane chaise or two. Nothing too smart or flashy. Delicately forged iron with matching chairs might look best in an enclosed space such as a walled courtyard or loggia. And if you like eating in different places in

ABOVE TOP: *Dense hedges and garden walls will help buffer noise while ensuring privacy. Disguise unsightly walls with ivy or top with a row of potted plants.*

ABOVE BOTTOM: *Pools and fountains are restful on the eyes and the sound of moving water soothes the senses. Pools also offer fun and refreshment for homeowners and visitors alike.*

OPPOSITE: *Outdoor furniture should be sturdy enough to withstand rain, wind, and sun. Wicker always looks good outdoors and the seats can be cushioned for extra comfort.*

RIGHT: *Porches look great furnished with a couch, a hammock or glider, rocking chairs, or a cane chaise like this one. Set small tables by chairs and couches to hold drinks, books, and so forth.*

OPPOSITE: *An outdoor fireplace is the ultimate in comfort. When lit, the fireplace will lend a warm glow to this entire dining area arranged in an ornamental grotto-like setting.*

## Comfort Zoning

### SEAT CUSHION COVERS BASICS

When you are having seat cushion covers made, get two or three made for easy laundering and match them with tablecloths and napkins. Find some cheerful color-coordinated scatter pillows as well, which always *look* comfortable, even if they are not.

a garden it is useful to keep a supply of portable card tables and folding chairs, if you have the storage space, and place them where the spirit and the mood of the day suggests. Unless that is, you feel able to afford permanent little groupings here and there. On the other hand, if you have a terrace by a pool, it is fun, if you have the funds, to buy some good-quality, beautifully designed new collections from Italy or Scandinavia or France, just as residents of those countries in their turn feel particularly sophisticated buying the best from the United States.

## ACCESSORIES

If you eat and drink out on your outdoor space a lot, it is worth getting some sort of side or serving table and some small tables to go by chairs for drinks, unless your chairs and chaises have in-built space for cool drinks, hors d'oeuvres, and books. Get tablecloths made with a reinforced hole in the middle so you can stick large market umbrellas through them without tearing the centers of the cloths. You can also make your chairs more comfortable by adding squab cushions. Coordinate or match these, too, to your general ensemble of table and seating covers. Look around your garden and terrace spaces too. Low walls make good bench areas, with the aid of long rectangles of thick foam rubber cut to fit. Cover them with gay washable cotton seat covers that can be zipped on and off in a minute.

## COMFORTING SMELLS

Good smells are as beguiling outside as anywhere else in the home. It is always good to plant sweet-smelling night flowers around the place: jasmine, nicotiana, and night-scented stocks are only a few of the many types of scented flowers commercially available. But when you barbeque, the smell of grilling meat will blanket any floral scents. So you might just as well make that smell more pleasant by throwing pieces of rosemary and thyme and apple or any other fruitwood on the coals and by burning particularly good-smelling woods in your outdoor fireplace (see page 42 for a list of woods).

## A FINAL THOUGHT

All in all, given the advantages of an outdoor space, however small (even if it is only a balcony outside an apartment), it behooves us to pay as much attention to the comfort of the exterior as to the interior. Such an area can be pleasing to all the senses, not least the olfactory kind. Any aesthetic improvements as well as any additions to physical well-being are so well worth the extra effort.

But then, so is attention to all things that can possibly add to comfort and contentment and security in a home, whether it be as simple as maintaining tidy drawers and well-ordered storage, or as time-consuming as choosing the most appropriate color schemes and furnishings and making sure that the lighting is exactly right in each area. One thing is for sure though—you will never ever regret *any* effort you make towards instilling comfort of whatever sort in your home.

## In Praise of Outdoor Fireplaces

Although it is somewhat of a luxury, if you have the space to install one, an outdoor fireplace is the ultimate in comfort. This is not only a cheerful thing to light when evenings turn chillier. It also means that you can probably extend your outdoor times by starting earlier in the spring and going on later into the fall. You might even be able to barbeque on it. (See pages 174–175 for sources of outdoor fireplaces.)

A DEEP, DARK GREEN can be quite a warm color in cool or cold climates, especially in living rooms, dining rooms, and libraries. However, green is a receding color and is commonly thought of as cool. It is especially restorative in high temperatures, conjuring up the pleasures of sheltering trees, dappled meadows, deep green-blue hills, fresh young leaves, damp tender moss, and the lovely juxtaposition of silvery green willow branches drooping into sun-dappled green-brown water. And, surprising for a color, it also conjures up smells along with vision: the sweetness of new-mown grass; the crisp, cool, apply crunch of a Granny Smith; the intoxicating freshness of leaves after a welcome rain; the invigorating scent of wet pine needles.

*Green conjures the pleasure and freshness of sheltering trees and rolling meadows. A profusion of potted plants can cool and invigorate a sunroom or patio, especially in warm climates.*

You can learn a great deal about creating comforting color schemes by scrutinizing and analyzing various painters' works. Because green is the predominant color in nature, painters have always been fascinated by the exercise of re-creating its various subtleties and moods. John Constable, that most lyrical of late eighteenth-century English landscape painters, is particularly worth a detailed examination. Eugène Delacroix, the great nineteenth-century French painter, thought so too. He recalled in his journal: "Constable says that the superiority of greens in his meadows is due to the fact that they are made up of a large number of *different* greens (juxtaposed, not mixed)."

Even a large glossy-leafed plant in a space will work wonders as a natural freshener. The same principle can be applied to interiors where a number of different greens gives a much more natural, living feel to a scheme rather than any single green used throughout. In one of Constable's sun-dappled water meadows, for example, you will find yellowy greens, gray greens, sludgy greens, reddish greens—and almost certainly the contrast of a white gate or building, the browny-gray of an old wood fence, the flash of a yellow buttercup, or the red of a poppy. Much the same kind of inspiration can come from studying the contrasts shown in the exuberant, exotic jungles of the brilliant French primitive painter Henri Rousseau, or in the sensual serenity of Claude Monet's water lily ponds. All these colors translate well into wall colors and accessories, and the general consensus could be that almost all greens provide a certain tranquility.

*Green is the color of nature. It translates well into wall and floor colors, and provides a certain tranquility and harmony when painted on the exterior of a home.*

THE STYLE OF YOUR OUTDOOR FURNITURE SHOULD FIT THE GENERAL LOOK OF YOUR HOUSE.

# Where to Go for What

*(E-mail or telephone for information and retailers near you.)*

**Important Note:** If any merchandise can only be sold through designers and readers are not using one, goods can always be bought through a Decor & You decorator near you. Contact: www.decorandyou.com, or (203) 264-3500.

## BATHTUBS, SHOWERS, AND SINKS
AMERICAN STANDARD:
   www.americanstandard-us.com
DURAVIT: www.duravit.com
HERBEAU CREATIONS: www.herbeau.com
JACUZZI: www.jacuzzi.com
KALLISTA: www.kallista.com
KOHLER: www.kohler.com (look at the new overflowing tub)
LEFROY BROOKS: www.lefroybrooks.com
P. E. GUERIN: www.peguerin.com
PHILIPPE STARCK: www.starck-bath.com
PORCHER: www.porcher-us.com
SHERLE WAGNER: www.sherlewagner.com
URBAN ARCHAEOLOGY:
   www.urbanarchaeology.com
WATERWORKS: www.waterworks.com, or (800) 899-6757

## BED LINENS, FEATHER PILLOWS, AND COMFORTERS
BONJOUR: www.bonswit.com
CALVIN KLEIN HOME: (212) 696-4646
FRETTE: through good bed linen stores and department stores
GARNETT HILL: (800) 622-6216 (flannel sheets)
HERMES: www.hermes.com, or (800) 441-4488 (Avalon wool cashmere throws)
HOTEL COLLECTION (at Macy's stores):
   www.macys.com, or (800) 417-2699
LEONTINE LINENS: www.leontinelinens.com
RALPH LAUREN: www.rlhome.polo.com
SIGNORIA LINENS: www.signoria.com
THE WHITE COMPANY: www.thewhiteco.com
TOMMY HILFIGER HOME: www.tommy.com, or (888) TOMMY4U
YVES DELORME: www.yvesdelorme.com

## BEDS
CHARLES P. ROGERS: www.charlesprogers.com, or (800) 272-7726
DREXEL-HERITAGE: www.drexelheritage.com, or (866) 450-3434
FLOU SALINA BEDS: www.flou.it, info@flou.qc.ca, or (310) 289-8717; (212) 941-9101 (combines excellent storage)

ROOM & BOARD: www.roomandboard.com, or (800) 486-6554
VERARDO/ITALIA: info@veradoitalia.it; also for distribution in North America: info@verstile.com, or (514) 327-6667

## CARPETS AND RUGS
ABC CARPET AND HOME: (212) 473-3000, ext. 400
COURISTAN: (800) 223-6186, ext. 523
KARASTAN: www.karastan.com, or (800) 234-1120
SAFAVIEH: (212) 477-1234, (203) 327-4800, or (201) 634-9800
STANTON CARPET: www.stantoncarpet.com
THE RUG COMPANY: www.therugcompany.info, or sales@therugcompany.info

## COUNTERTOP MATERIALS
BUDDY RHODES CONCRETE: (415) 641-8070
COLD SPRINGS GRANITE:
   www.coldspringgranite.com
DUPONT CORIAN: www.corian.com, or (800) 4CORIAN
ESKAY METAL FABRICATING STAINLESS STEEL:
   www.specialtystainless.com
GREEN MOUNTAIN SOAPSTONE:
   www.greenmountainsoapstone.com
JOHN BOOS BUTCHER BLOCK:
   www.johnboos.com
OKITE: www.okite.com (engineered stone)
PYROLAVE ENAMELED LAVASTONE:
   www.pyrolave.com
SHELDON SLATE: www.sheldonslate.com
ZODIAQ: www.zodiaq.com (engineered stone)

## DISHWASHERS
ASKO: www.askousa.com
BOSCH: www.boschappliances.com
DACOR: www.dacor.com
FISHER & PAYKEL: www.fisherpaykel.com
GE: www.geappliances.com
JENN-AIR: www.jennair.com
KITCHENAID: www.kitchenaid.com
MIELE: www.miele.com
SUB ZERO: www.subzero.com
VIKING: www.vikingrange.com
WHIRLPOOL: www.whirlpool.com

## FEATHER MATTRESSES
L. L. BEAN: www.llbean.com

## FLOOR TILES
ANN SACKS: www.annsacks.com
ARTISTIC TILES: www.artistictile.com

COUNTRY FLOORS: www.countryfloors.com
PARIS CERAMICS: www.parisceramics.com
STONE SOURCE: www.stonesource.com
STUDIUM: www.studiumnyc.com, or (212) 486-1811
WALKER ZANGER: www.walkerzanger.com
WATERWORKS: www.waterworks.com

## HARD FLOORS (for kitchens)
AMTICO: www.amtico.com
ARMSTRONG: www.armstrong.com
MOHAWK HARD SURFACE:
   www.mohawk-laminateflooring.com
PERGO: www.pergo.com
WILSONART: www.wilsonart.com

## HARDWOOD FLOORS
(see also Floor Tiles)
MIRAGE: www.miragefloors.com, or (800) 463-1303 (prefinished hardwood floors)
PIANETA LEGNO: www.plfloors.com, or (866) 753-5667

## HEATING, COOLING, AND AIR PURIFYING SYSTEMS
DAVE LENNOX SIGNATURE SYSTEMS:
   www.lennox.com, or (800) 9-Lennox
JENN-AIR: www.jennair.com, or (800) JENN-AIR (kitchen air extraction)

## KITCHEN CABINETS
BOFFI: www.boffi.com
BULTHAUP: www.bulthaup.com
CHRISTOPHER PEACOCK CABINETRY:
   www.peacockcabinetry.com
CLIVE CHRISTIAN: 011 44 1204 702 216
POGGENPOHL: www.poggenpohl-usa.com
RUTT HANDCRAFTED CABINETRY: www.rutt.net
SMALLBONE: www.smallbone.co.uk
SIEMATIC: www.siematic.com
ST. CHARLES: through retail outlets
WOOD-MODE: www.wood-mode.com

## KITCHEN CHAIR UPHOLSTERY AND TABLECLOTH FABRICS
(spill-proof/stain-proof)
CRYPTON TEXTILES COTTON TWILLS,
   DISTRIBUTED BY ROBERT ALLEN:
   www.robertallendesign.com.
   (through designers only or through Decor & You: www.decorandyou.com, or (203) 264-3500)

## KITCHEN EQUIPMENT
WILLIAMS-SONOMA: www.williams-sonoma.com
   (more than 200 stores)

# Bibliography

**KITCHEN SINKS**
BLANCO: www.blancoamerica.com
ELKAY: www.elkayusa.com
FRANKE: www.frankeksd.com
GERMAN SILVER SINK:
  www.germansilversink.com
HERBEAU CREATIONS: www.herbeau.com
KALLISTA: www.kallista.com
KINDRED: www.kindred-sinkware.com
KOHLER'S PREP TROUGH SINK: www.kohler.com
WATERWORKS: www.waterworks.com

**LIGHTING**
ARTEMIDE: www.artemide.us, or (631) 694-9292
LOUIS POULSEN: www.louispoulsen.com, or
  (954) 349-2525
OGGETTI LUCE: www.oggetti.com, or
  (305) 576-1044
THOMAS O'BRIEN DESIGNS FOR VISUAL
  COMFORT: www.visualcomfort.com, or
  (877) 271-2716

**OUTDOOR FURNITURE**
GIATI: www.giati.com (teak and hand-cast
  metal furniture; market umbrellas)
GLOSTER: www.gloster.com, or (888) GLOSTER
GRANGE: www.grange.fr, or (800) GRANGE-1
KINGSLEY-BATE: www.kingsleybate.com, or
  (703) 361-7000 (solid teak)
WALPOLE WOODWORKERS:
  www.walpolewoodworkers.com,
  or (800) 343-6948

**PAINTS**
BEHR: www.behr.com
BENJAMIN MOORE: www.benjaminmoore.com
DISNEY FOR CHILDREN'S ROOMS: through retail
  outlets
GLIDDEN: www.glidden.com
PRATT & LAMBERT: (800) BUY-PRATT
RALPH LAUREN: www.rlhome.polo.com
THE HOME DEPOT/COLOR SOLUTIONS
  CENTER COLORSMART SYSTEM:
  www.homedepot.com/colorsolutions

**REFRIGERATORS**
GE: www.geappliances.com
JENN-AIR: www.jennair.com
KITCHENAID: www.kitchenaid.com
SUB ZERO: www.subzero.com (take a look at
  the under-the-counter Sub Zero 700 BC
  with refrigerator and freezer drawers)
TRAULSEN: www.traulsen.com

**STOVES AND COOK TOPS**
AGA: www.aga-ranges.com
DACOR: www.dacor.com

GAGGENAU: www.gaggenau.com
GARLAND: www.garland-group.com
LA CORNUE: www.lacornue.com
MIELE: www.miele.com
THERMADOR: www.thermador.com
VIKING: www.vikingrange.com
WOLF: www.subzero.com/wolf, or
  (800) 444-7820

**UPHOLSTERY**
ARMANI CASA, NYC: (212) 334-1271
B&B ITALIA: (800) 872-1697
BAKER, KNAPP & TUBBS: through designers,
  or at the New York Design Center,
  200 Lexington Avenue, Suite 300,
  New York, NY
CASSINA USA: (800) 770-3568
DE SEDE: www.desede.com, or
  infousa@desede.com
DOMUS DESIGN COLLECTION (DDC):
  www.ddcnyc.com, or (212) 685-0800
EKORNES FAMILY MEDIA COLLECTION:
  www.ekornes.com, office@ekornes.com,
  or (888) EKORNES
HENREDON: www.henredon.com
KRAVET: www. decorandyou.com, or through
  designers
LIGNE ROSET: (800) BY-ROSET
MAURICE VILLENCY: (212) 725-4840
MINOTTI S.P.A: www.minotti.com, or
  info@minotti.it
MITCHELL GOLD: www.mitchellgold.com, or
  (800) 789-5401
RALPH LAUREN HOME'S CANYON WOVEN
  LEATHER CHAISE: (888) 475-7674
ROCHE-BOBOIS: (800) 972-8375
SUMMIT FURNITURE INC.:
  www.summitfurniture.com
TODD OLDHAM BY LAZBOY:
  www.lazboy.com/oldham

**WALL TILES**
ANN SACKS: www.annsacks.com
ARTISTIC TILES: www.artistictile.com
BISAZZA NORTH AMERICA: www.bisazzausa.com
CERAMIC TILES OF ITALY: www.italiatiles.com,
  or (212) 980-1500
COUNTRY FLOORS: www.countryfloors.com
HASTINGS TILE: www.hastingstilebath.com
STONE SOURCE: www.stonesource.com
STUDIUM: www.studiumnyc.com, or
  (212) 486-1811
URBAN ARCHAEOLOGY:
  www.urbanarchaeology.com
WALKER ZANGER:
  www.walkerzanger.com
WATERWORKS: www.waterworks.com

Conran, Terence, with Elaine Greene.
  *Terence Conran's The New House Book.*
  London: Conran Octopus, 1999.
Gilliatt, Mary. *English Country Style.* Boston:
  Little, Brown, 1986.
———. *The Mary Gilliatt Book of Color.*
  Boston: Little, Brown, 1985.
———. *Period Style.* Boston: Little, Brown,
  1990.
———, and Douglas Baker. *Lighting Your
  Home: A Practical Guide.* New York:
  Pantheon Books,1979.
Hampton, Mark. *Mark Hampton on
  Decorating.* New York: Random House,
  1989.
Hills, Nicholas. *The English Fireplace
  (Its Architecture and the Working Fire).*
  London: Quiller Press, 1983.
McCorquodale, Charles. *History of the
  Interior.* London: The Vendome Press,
  1983.
Rybczynski, Witold. *Home: A Short History
  of an Idea.* New York: Viking Penguin,
  1986.
Watkin, David. *A History of Western
  Architecture.* London: Lawrence King
  Publishing, 1992.

# Index